THE OUTLAWS
OF SUCCESS

THE OUTLAWS OF SUCCESS

Bending The Rules
Without Crossing The Line

**Larry Winget • Dale Irvin
Scott McKain • Mark Sanborn
John Patrick Dolan**

THE OUTLAWS OF SUCCESS

Bending The Rules Without Crossing The Line

Larry Winget • Dale Irvin • Scott McKain
Mark Sanborn • John Patrick Dolan

Copyright ©MCMXCIX

Printed in the United States Of America.

Cover design and layout by Ad Graphics, Tulsa, Oklahoma.
800.368.6196
www.adgraf.com

Cover photography by Jean Phillippe, Dallas, Texas

ISBN: 1-881342-23-9

Published by:

THE HOLE IN THE WALL PRESS

P. O. Box 700485
Tulsa, Oklahoma 74170

MORE FROM THE OUTLAWS

The Outlaws have many other products.
For more information contact any of
The Outlaws individually at the numbers below.

Larry Winget
800.749.4597

Dale Irvin
800.951.7321

Scott McKain
800.297.5844

Mark Sanborn
800.650.3343

John Patrick Dolan
800.859.0888

TABLE OF CONTENTS

CHAPTER 1

ATTITUDE ISN'T EVERYTHING & MOTIVATION DOESN'T WORK

. . . .

by Larry Winget, CSP

ATTITUDE ISN'T EVERYTHING & MOTIVATION DOESN'T WORK

by Larry Winget, CSP

■ ■ ■ ■ ■ ■ ■ ■ ■ ■ ■ ■ ■ ■ ■ ■

"What??????? How can you say that? You lie! You are a bad man! I buy books by motivational speakers all the time! I go hear motivational speakers whenever I get a chance. I listen to motivational tapes and am Nightingale-Conant's biggest and best customer. So what do you mean attitude isn't everything and motivation doesn't work?"

Well, let me prove it to you. If you are the kind of person who does what was just described in the first paragraph (or since you are the kind of person who bought this book) then answer these questions: How is your life? Are you rich, happy, healthy and successful? No? Well, there you go, that stuff doesn't really work does it? (By the way, if you really are rich, happy, healthy and successful, then congratulations. But it wasn't the motivation that worked, it was you.)

13

Don't you just hate that? You're caught. Now don't feel bad. I used to be just like you. I have read over a thousand motivational, self-help books. I have also listened to at least that many motivational, self-help tapes. I have also been to lots of meetings and heard the high-powered, high-priced, motivational gurus say all that cool stuff about feeling good about yourself. I have listened to them tell the masses to just have a good attitude and anything will be possible. I would sit on the edge of my seat and eat it up until I would nearly swoon with the idea that if only I had the right attitude my life would be okay.

Listen, I've had a good positive attitude all my life and I've had more crap happen to me than you can imagine! I had a great attitude and went bankrupt. I had a great attitude the whole time I had problems in my business, in my relationships, with my money and my health. That wonderful positive attitude of mine didn't keep one thing from happening to me.

So regardless of what any of the books, tapes and speakers say, attitude isn't everything. I know that's a lot to swallow since it flies in the face of what everyone else says and everything you have ever heard. But attitude isn't everything. Like you, I've seen books out there telling you that attitude is everything. Did you know that you can buy a cute little rock to use as a paper weight (like you have paper that needs a weight!) that says

"ATTITUDE IS EVERYTHING?" You can even get little coins to carry in your pocket to remind you of the same sentiment. And posters to line your walls. Isn't all of that just precious? Well sure it is, and it makes the suckers feel better and lines the pockets of the manufacturers. And it is still a lie because Attitude Isn't Everything!

Attitude is important, I'll give you that. Having a good attitude in fact is critical. But it won't keep anything from happening to you. It will help you deal with what happens to you but it won't keep anything from happening to you. So it is important, I do admit that. But it certainly isn't everything. Attitude is only one thing.

Attitude will help you deal with what happens to you but it won't keep anything from happening to you.

What people sometimes think is that if they get their attitude right then they won't have problems, they won't have anything bad happen to them, and they won't even have to work, simply because their attitude is so good.

Well the real truth is that sooner or later you have to get off your pie-in-the-sky fanny and do some work!

That's right—work! A dirty word. But you have to understand that you are paid for effort. The effort to serve others well. Service is rewarded. Always. It is a Universal Law. Earl Nightingale said, "Your rewards in life are in direct proportion to your service." Service comes disguised as work. I will give you this much on attitude: you must perform your service/work with a good attitude. But even service/work performed with a bad attitude gets rewarded. Attitude doesn't get you paid, work gets you paid. Work performed with a good attitude will get you paid better and make the work go faster and will definitely be more fun, but the key ingredient to doing well is still the work, the effort, the service!

> **Attitude doesn't get you paid, work gets you paid.**

Hey, you've been to the seminars, I'll bet you've heard this one:

We are not human doings, we are human beings.

What a load of crap that is. But you have heard all the motivational hot shots say that one haven't you?

Why do you think they say it? It sells, that's why. I have even said it myself. I am not proud of it but I have...forgive me, even I sold out a few times.

The idea behind that statement is that people should focus more on who they are rather than what they do— that we have become a nation so caught up in doing that we have forgotten the importance of being. Bull. It sounds good but it isn't true. The truth is that we are not a nation of doers, we are a nation of watchers. We sit on our big fat butts and watch television. We like to say that we are doers, but face it, the few do, the many watch. And all the many who watch can do is gripe about the few who do because it should have been done differently.

We are not a nation of doers, we are a nation of watchers!

However, that's why we like that statement so much. It gets us off the hook for not doing anything. It tells us to forget the doing and focus on the being. I love the idea that we should focus on being better people. Of course we should. We should all become as good as we can. We should become as spiritual as we can, as smart as we can, as loving as we can, as healthy as we can, as successful as we can, as rich as we can, and on and on and on. But will we? Most never will. Why? Effort. It takes effort to be spiritual, smart, loving, healthy, successful, rich, and the rest. That why so few achieve any of those things. They won't put out the effort. They want to think themselves into a better life. Or contemplate their way to a better life. It won't work.

You can sit under a tree and contemplate your navel until the end of eternity, and until you get up, dust your butt off and go do something, very little is going to change.

I am not playing down the importance of meditation, quiet time, prayer, introspection, whatever it is you want to call it or how you want to practice it. I do it myself. It is a wonderful thing. However, the purpose of those acts is to bring about clarity of purpose; to make clearer what we are destined to do once we stand back up; to bring into focus our way of serving others through our efforts.

So if you want to have a better life...DO SOMETHING!

I believe that we have forgotten our English lessons. Actually that's pretty obvious, just listen to the conversations around you. It sounds like most people never even had an English lesson, much less remember their lessons. Them people ain't got no idea how to talk good irregardless of what they been learnt.

So let's look again at an old English lesson. Remember state of being verbs? Sure you do. Well, maybe you don't. The state of being verbs are: is, are, am, was, and were. They reflect our "state of being." They do NOT reflect any state of action. That's what you were taught in elementary school. However, we sell those state of being verbs just a bit short. Because they actually do reflect action. Let me show you: If you are, you must do. Because anything that is, does. So if you don't, then you aren't.

> **If you are, you must do.**
> **Because anything that is, does.**
> **So if you don't, then you aren't.**

Are you? Of course you are. And since you are, you must do. I'm not implying that you aren't doing something. You are doing something. You are watching television, eating too much, griping…but why am I telling you? Look at your day and make your own list!

So it's not that you aren't doing, you are doing. You just aren't doing anything productive. You aren't serving anyone. You aren't helping anyone. You aren't really doing anything except sitting on your butt and watching the world go by. That big cruel world that treats you bad and keeps you broke and unhappy. So due to your lack of doing the right things, you aren't really success-ful. You aren't rich. You aren't happy. So fix it! Do something—do the right things.

What are the right things? I don't need to tell you. You know what they are. You aren't a complete idiot are you? You know exactly what you need to do to change your life completely for the better. The problem is never that we don't know, it is always that we don't do what we already know.

The problem is never that we don't know, it is always that we don't do what we already know.

So I am not going to insult you by making you a cute little list that says "just do this stuff" and you'll be okay. Besides, I have already done that in my other books. So if you want lists of things to do to have a better life, buy my book, *Just Do This Stuff*. It has lists of things to do in over thirty areas of personal and professional life. And it's cheap. The phone call is even free: 800.749.4597. But how many people who say that they really want to do better are really going to pick up the phone and get the book? Very few. How sad.

So am I totally against motivation and self-help? Not at all. I make my living in that industry. But look at those two concepts: motivation and self-help. People think of those as separate things. The key is to put those two concepts together. The only way to become motivated is to help yourself. It is up to you. Not up to a book, or a tape, or a speech. None of those things can really motivate you. So don't look to them. Don't count on them. Sounds strange to hear that from a guy who has written fifteen self-help books and recorded lots of audio and video tapes, and gives speeches for a living doesn't it? It may sound strange but the truth often does. I don't believe that any book or tape or speech can really motivate you. Those things can only help you to motivate yourself. You will only change when you are ready to and want to and believe that you can. A book, a tape, or a speaker only serves you well when it makes you believe that you can. And most motivation isn't known for that. Instead, most motivation is known for making you feel good about who you are. Feeling good about yourself won't move you from where you are to where you want to be.

That's why I say that motivation doesn't work. If it did, then motivational speakers would run the world and they would be zillionaires. Trust me, they don't run the world and they aren't zillionaires. Except for Tony Robbins. I don't underestimate the value of what some motivational speakers say. I owe a lot to many of them.

But I don't owe any of them for teaching me that feeling good about who I am will make a difference. I do however owe a great deal to those who reminded me instead to feel good about what I can do.

That's what you need to understand. Motivation that makes you feel good about yourself won't change your life. Knowing that you can do whatever you want to do will change your life. You have to move from feeling good about yourself to believing in yourself. There is a major difference between the two concepts. Who cares if you feel good about yourself? Instead, believe in yourself. That belief will propel you to amazing heights. You will believe that you can do whatever you want to do. And you can!

Motivation that makes you feel good about yourself won't change your life. Knowing that you can do whatever you want to do will change your life.

Most speakers and most books and tapes teach the concept backwards. Even I have taught it backwards in some of my other books, tapes, and speeches. That doesn't really matter. Very few read the books, even fewer do what the books say. Lots of people buy them, but few read them or follow the advice. So it doesn't matter if I said something wrong.

Many of us have said that in order to have, you must do. And in order to do, you must be. In other words, if I feel good about who I am, then I will be able to do anything.

Heard that before? Sure you have. Well, that might work. Yeah, in a fairy tale world that might work. Our society won't let you feel good about who you are. You are constantly reminded that you just aren't good enough. Well, know what? It's true. You aren't. So face it. You aren't good enough to do whatever you want to do. But should that stop you? Hell no. You have to do it anyway. You are never going to feel that you have enough going for you to accomplish anything you want to accomplish. Does that mean you can't do it? Does it mean that you can't accomplish what you want to accomplish? Absolutely not. You can do whatever you want to do. But you won't do it by feeling good about yourself. You will only do it by doing it. You just have to start. You have to do it and do it and do it. You have to do it badly. You have to do anything, even something pitifully small in order to give yourself the courage to do a little more. That's how things get done. Things get done by doing something, not by feeling good about who you are. So do something. Anything. Even if you do the wrong thing, you'll find out quicker than by not doing anything at all. So do it. Get started. Now.

Things get done by doing something, not by feeling good about who you are.

Motivational speakers will tell you that the key is self-image. The key is not self-image. Self-image is based on the words "I am." How I feel about myself based on who I am. Well face it. You are not who you want to be. Whaaaa! Too bad. Why don't you just sit in the corner and whine about it. Maybe Oprah or Jesse or Jerry will have you on their shows so you can get the whole world to feel sorry for you. Whine about it instead of taking responsibility for it. That'll help.

How you feel about who you are just isn't that important. How you feel about what you "can do" is what is important. The key is self-CAN-age. I made that word up. Isn't it cool? My word is based on how you feel about yourself based on what you can do. And you can do anything.

I don't give one hoot about what "you am." The only thing important is what "you can." Once again, you can do anything. People have done amazing things. I can show you people with tremendous difficulties to overcome and yet they still accomplish the most incredible things. So it just doesn't matter who you are or how you feel about who you are. Because you rarely feel good enough about yourself to do amazing things. The important thing is to know, without a doubt, that you can do amazing things.

Not perfectly. At least not to begin with. But when you begin with a little you can build the courage to do more. And with that courage you can do a little more. And then a little more. And then a little more until it is done and something amazing has been accomplished.

That's why motivation doesn't work. Motivation typically says that some force outside of yourself will inspire you to feel good enough about yourself so you will be able to do anything your little heart desires. Forget it. Instead, I say that in order to do anything your little heart desires, you must know that you can do anything because if it has ever been done by anyone at any time then you too can do it. Because no one is special. It's just that some people have the courage to begin and are willing to risk failure and are willing to continue doing it until it gets done.

Big difference. That's why I don't call myself a motivational speaker. I don't believe I can motivate you to feel good enough about yourself to do anything. Instead, I call myself an irritational speaker. Actually, I am The World's Only Irritational Speaker™. I believe that given enough time I can make you so irritated with your results in life that you will be willing to risk anything in order to be more, do more and have more. And I'll do that by proving to you that you can do whatever you want.

My approach won't make you feel good. And I know how important it is to you to feel good. But feeling good never got you to do anything. If you listen to a speaker who makes you feel good I doubt you will ever do a thing. If you listen to a speaker who makes you feel uncomfortable, then you might do something.

For instance, about 70% of our society is overweight. Don't believe me? Look down. As an overweight person, you might get all dressed up, look in the mirror and say to yourself, "You know, I look pretty good!" As long as you convince yourself that you look good and you feel good about yourself, then you are never going to lose weight. It's on the day that you are walking past the mirror with your gut and your butt hanging out and you stop and say to yourself, "Damn, I'm HUGE!" That's when you are going to do something. Why? Because you AREN'T comfortable with yourself—you don't feel good about yourself. And what about when you are walking past someone you love and trust and THEY say to you, "Damn, you are HUGE!" Then, I'll guarantee you will do something. Because THAT is motivation!

Think of me as that trusted loved one who just caught you walking past all naked and hanging out—and know that I am telling you, "You are HUGE!" Because my goal is to make you uncomfortable. Because if you are uncomfortable then you will change.

Feeling good does not create change. Uncomfortable-ness creates change. Why do you change your position in your chair? Because the position you are in is uncomfortable and you are changing it to get more comfortable. If you weren't uncomfortable in your current position then you wouldn't move—you would just stay where you are.

> **Feeling good does not create change.**
> **Uncomfortable-ness creates change.**

I want to make you uncomfortable. I want my words to make you uncomfortable. Why? Because I want you to change. I want you to find your best self and go for it. I want you to believe in what you are able to do, to create, to accomplish, and to achieve.

I want to give you a focus and a direction. I want to encourage you to do something. I want you to take action. But it has to be action focused toward what you really want. Not the kind of action that has you running around like a chicken with its head cut off. (By the way, isn't that the stupidest expression you ever heard? Other than "that's the best thing since sliced bread." What about computers, space travel, plastic, movies, and stuff like that? Isn't that better than sliced bread?)

Typically, motivation is a lot like blowing up a balloon. You blow the balloon up and without tying the end of it, you let it go and it flies all over the room banging into everything. While it is great to have a balloon all blown up to play with, to really enjoy it you have to tie the end off so you can really have some fun with it. You can use it like a ball or rub it on your head and let the static electricity stick it to the wall. Or you can tie a string to it and anchor it to something and bat it around. Without tying off the end you have the frustration of just blowing it up over an over and over again until it finally blows out the window or pops.

Watch people who have just gotten all fired up and motivated and yet haven't been given any direction. They are like the balloon. They bounce around the room letting out lots of motivational hot air passing out "ATTITUDE IS EVERYTHING" buttons and getting in everyone's way. They have no direction.

I watched my son, Tyler, graduate from basic training in the Army. After the ceremony when they were doing their yells and cheers and all that Army stuff, one of the Sergeants yelled out, "Are you motivated?!?!?!" At which point they all yelled in unison, " Motivated, motivated, down-right motivated, you check us out, you check us out!!!!!!!!!!" When I asked him about all of that, he said that they all yelled that out at the beginning of any task, assignment or exercise. Now what is critical to understand is that they already knew the assignment, the task or the exercise inside and out before they started yelling about how motivated they were. To yell about being motivated with no clue about the task would have been stupid. Why get motivated without a plan? They had a plan, they knew how to do it, then they got motivated to accomplish it.

Do you see how that is the way we should do it? You must have the plan first. To get motivated without a plan is stupid. You are nothing but a balloon full of hot air.

I believe you must have direction: plans, dreams, desires, a picture of what you want, how much you want, who you want and how you want it to be. You don't need pages of plans, you just need a direction that can be articulated and focused on so you can direct your energy toward it.

You may be saying I don't know exactly what I want. Let me help you. It's probably what you don't have. So look around and take stock.

Ask yourself if this is how you want to live your life. Is it? Then why are you living this way? Don't you deserve better? Of course you do. Can you have better? Of course you can. Everyone can. If anyone can, everyone can. If anyone has ever done it, then you can do it. So go for it. You can do it.

Larry's Plan For A Better Life
■■■■■■■■■■■■■■■■■■■■■■■■■■■■

1. Decide what you want.

2. Decide you deserve it.

3. Decide you can have it.

4. Focus your energy toward it.

5. Do something toward making it happen.

6. Keep doing more until it happens.

Seem too simple? It is simple. It's not easy though. This takes effort.

First, the DECISION. Good things rarely interrupt you. You have to decide what you want and decide you deserve it and decide that you can have it. Make the decision to have a better life. The decision alone will help bring you the courage to begin.

Focus your energy. Write down what you want out of life. Say it out loud to yourself. Think about it often. Read about it. Talk about it. Energy has an amazing effect on making things happen. When you do these things you will attract the thing you want to you. Trust me—it's a cosmic thing.

Then DO SOMETHING. I have spent about two thousand words on this one. So just get started.

Keep doing something. If the first thing you try doesn't work, then try it again. If it still doesn't work, try something else. Ask for help. But don't stop. You may give up right before your breakthrough.

Now you are ready. You are ready to get started on the road to a better life. Is this method foolproof? Will it work every time? Nope. You can do everything I say and sometimes this stuff still won't work. Why? Beats me. But I will make you this guarantee: You will get better results by doing it than by not doing it.

And if you find a better way, write a book and send it to me along with an invoice. I'll try your method next time. Just don't tell me it's motivational.

WANTED

6'0"

5'6"

5'0"

LARRY WINGET

LARRY WINGET, CSP

Larry Winget is a philosopher of success who just happens to be hilarious. He teaches universal principles that will work for anyone, in any business, at any time, and does it by telling funny stories. He believes that most of us have complicated life and business way too much, take it way too seriously and that we need to lighten up, take responsibility, be more flexible, stay positive and keep it in perspective. He believes that success and prosperity come from serving others. He teaches that business improves when the people in the business improve; that everything in life gets better when we get better and nothing gets better until we get better.

To have Larry speak to your organization or to order any of his other personal and professional development products contact:

Win Seminars! Inc.
P. O. Box 700485 • Tulsa, Oklahoma 74170
918.745.6606 • 800.749.4597
Fax: 918.747.3185

or use the Internet: www.larrywinget.com

LARRY WINGET ORDER FORM

Books

	Unit Cost	Quantity	Amount
The Simple Way To Success	$12.95	_____	_____
Money Is Easy	$11.95	_____	_____
Stuff That Works Every Single Day	$ 9.95	_____	_____
The Little Red Book Of Stuff That Works	$ 7.95	_____	_____
Just Do This Stuff	$ 7.95	_____	_____
Only The Best On Success	$11.95	_____	_____
Only The Best On Customer Service	$11.95	_____	_____
Only The Best On Leadership	$11.95	_____	_____
Success One Day At A Time	$11.95	_____	_____
That Makes Me Sick!	$ 7.95	_____	_____
Profound Stuff	$ 9.95	_____	_____
Outlaw Wisdom	$ 9.95	_____	_____
The Outlaws Of Success	$12.95	_____	_____
Larry's Library (all THIRTEEN above)	$100.00	_____	_____

Other Stuff

Shut Up! Stop Whining And Get A Life *cards* (50)	$ 9.95	_____	_____
Shut Up! Stop Whining And Get A Life ... *Coffee Mug*	$ 9.95	_____	_____
Stuff That Works ...*Mouse Pad*	$10.95	_____	_____
Shut Up! Stop Whining And Get A Life ... *Mouse Pad*	$10.95	_____	_____

UNGAWA GEAR

Shut Up, Stop Whining And Get A Life *T-shirt (XL only)*	$17.95	_____	_____
NMOD ƎꓒISꓒU version of above *T-shirt (XL only)*	$17.95	_____	_____
Shut Up, Stop Whining And Get A Life *hat*	$16.95	_____	_____
LWO – Larry World Order *T-shirt (XL only)*	$17.95	_____	_____

SHIPPING & HANDLING

If Sub Total is:	USA	Canada
0 - 25.00	$3.00	$ 10.00
25.01 - 100.00	$8.00	$20.00
100.01 - 200.00	$15.00	$30.00
200.01 - 300.00	$25.00	$40.00
Call for rates on purchases over $300.		

ALL PRICES U.S. DOLLARS
Canadian Shipping Rates do not include duty, taxes or customs charges that COULD be charged at the border

Sub Total _____

S&H _____

TOTAL _____

Name _____ Date _____

Company _____

STREET Address _____

City/Province _____

Zip/Postal Code _____ Country _____ Day Phone _____

Method of Payment: ☐ AMEX ☐ VISA ☐ Mastercard ☐ Check/Money Order Enclosed

Card No. | | | | | | | | | | | | | | | |

Exp. date _____ Signature _____

Win Seminars! Inc.
P. O. Box 700485 • Tulsa, Oklahoma 74170
918.745.6606 • 800.749.4597 • Fax: 918.747.3185
www.larrywinget.com

LAUGHTER, ANOTHER KEY TO OUTLAW SUCCESS

■ ■ ■ ■ ■ ■ ■ ■ ■ ■ ■ ■ ■ ■ ■ ■ ■ ■

by Dale Irvin, CSP, CPAE

Laughter, Another Key To Outlaw Success

by Dale Irvin, CSP, CPAE

■ ■ ■ ■ ■ ■ ■ ■ ■ ■ ■ ■ ■ ■ ■ ■ ■ ■

> **"White man speak with forked tongue—
> must be hard for him to eat soup."**
> **– Tonto**

W hen you are an outlaw, your job is to break the rules. This is clearly stated on page 16 of the Outlaw Instruction Manual right after the section on how to dress. ("Black hats are perfect for any occasion from a daylight bank robbery to a midnight lynching.")

One unwritten rule that we seem to over emphasize is that "business is serious business." We sometimes forget that it is possible to combine work and fun to create a healthier company, happier employees, and a bigger bottom line. An important rule to break when you are an outlaw is any rule that tells you not to have fun on your job. Unless you are an international terrorist or a serial killer, your job should be fun. You should enjoy doing it and look forward to it every day. This is possible you know, if you add a little laughter into your work place.

Over the rest of this chapter, I have outlined some ideas on how you can put more fun and laughter into your job and into your life, but what makes me laugh may not make you laugh. That's OK. All I want to do is to make you think about laughing more every day. It is up to you to think of ways to make it happen. For starters, let me tell you a little story about some real outlaws from the real old west who had a gunfight in a corral that was O.K.

The Gunfight At The OK Corral
The Real Story

The Gunfight at the OK Corral was fought on October 26, 1881 in Tombstone, Arizona which had recently won the AAA award for the Worst Name For A City narrowly edging out "Eviscerated Road Kill, Wyoming" and "Smells Like Crap Here, Nevada." At the time, Tombstone was a major tourist destination where westward bound families would stop to visit the Giant Water Slide, the House Of Wonder, and of course, the OK Corral.

The OK Corral was located next to the Okey Dokey Stable and right across the street from the All-Righty-Then Cafe. It was a very positive part of town. "The

Corral" as the locals called it, was the site of intense gang rivalry between The Clanton Gang and The Good Guys. The Clanton Gang consisted of Ike and Billy Clanton, Tom and Frank McLaury, and Billy Claiborn. Billy Claiborn had no brothers and he forbade his sister from joining the gang fearing that she would become a "gang ho."

The Good Guys were comprised of Marshall Virgil Earp and his brothers Morgan and Wyatt, plus their alcoholic friend "Doc" Holliday. Contrary to popular belief, "Doc" Holliday was not a medical doctor at all but had a Ph.D. in English Literature. He still performed surgery but he was very inexpensive.

The Clanton Gang wanted the turf of The Corral to operate their illegal rustling activities. In the fall of the year they would rake all of the town's leaves into the corral and rustle around in them. This created a big ruckus in town as the Clantons only allowed gang members to rustle in the leaves while the rest of the town was forced to go rustle-less. The Good Guys were in favor of open rustling and were very key in the passing of the Freedom Of Rustling Act. The Clanton Gang ignored this statute and vowed that no one caught rustling in their corral would get out alive. This brings us to the fateful day, October 26, 1881.

The town was in severe dismay as they realized that Halloween was fast approaching, and, while cornstalks and pumpkins were in ample supply, there was not a single leaf of color available for their holiday decorating needs. They approached Marshall Virgil and demanded that something be done. Virgil phoned up his brothers who were busy working on their new brew pub ("Earp Beer, It Tastes As Good As It Sounds") and told them to get "Doc" and get ready to rumble.

At approximately 2:05 PM Mountain Time (4:05 Eastern) the Good Guys entered the OK Corral and met the Clanton Gang. The ensuing scene went something like this...

Virgil: Hey you Clantons, get out of the Corral, OK?

"Doc": I believe the correct name is OK Corral.

Virgil: Oh, listen to Mister I-Have-A-College-Degree. All right, have it your way. Hey you Clantons, get out of the OK Corral, OK?

Clantons: *rustle, rustle, rustle.*

Virgil: Doggone it Clantons, stop rustling right now and fight like a man.

"Doc": I don't mean to sound picky, but since we are dealing with a plural subject here, I think the correct term is "fight like *men.*"

Clantons: *rustle, rustle, rustle.*

Wyatt:	If this ever gets made into a TV series, I'd like Hugh O'Brien to play me.
Morgan:	How about in the movies?
Wyatt:	Anybody but Kevin Costner.
Virgil:	That's it Clantons, I'm taking back this corral.
SFX:	Assorted gun shots, mixed with rustling, taunting, and the occasional "F" word.

The fight at the OK Corral ended that day with some dead guys lying in the leaves which really cut down on the town's eagerness to rustle in the pile. Ike Clanton escaped the carnage and went on to marry Tina Turner. Wyatt Earp achieved his dream of Hugh O'Brien portraying him on TV but unfortunately he had been dead for 75 years before it happened. On the bright side, he wasn't alive to see Kevin Costner's portrayal in the movie.

"Doc" Holliday went on to perform heart transplants and penile enhancement surgery while Morgan Earp took up performance art and became the first mime of the old west. He was beaten to death with sticks.

And now for the $20,000 question,[1] did that story make you laugh? Did it make you smile? Did it make you want to smile but you are reading it in church during

---

[1] This is meant as a euphemism based on a television game show from the 60's. If you paid $20,000 for this book you were terribly over charged.

the service and you don't' want anybody to see that you are smiling? If your answer to any of the above is "Huh?", you are ready to break the rules by having more fun at work and at home. Here are some outlaw tips to help you get started.

OUTLAW LAUGHTER TIP #1

When The Going Gets Tough…
The Tough Tell Jokes

Have you ever had one of those days? You know the kind—you overslept, you have a headache, you are out of coffee, the dog pooped in the living room, you forgot to pick up the dry cleaning and now have nothing to wear, the car won't start, you have noticeably less hair on your head than you did yesterday, and the video rental store charged you extra because you didn't rewind. We have all had one of these days. They are unavoidable setbacks on the road of life. In the words of the famous philosopher Confucius, "S**T HAPPENS!"[2]

If we accept the fact that S**T is going to happen to us sooner or later, we can prepare for it and plan a strategy. My suggestion is take care of the S**T through the elevated use of laughter.

---

[2] Actually, Confucius said "Spit Happens" but I did not feel comfortable mentioning saliva.

The stress that accompanies the trials of everyday life can be dealt with in one of two ways. You can allow it to make you tense, hypertensive, nervous, and cause the heartbreak of psoriasis. (Actually, I'm not too sure about that last one but you can look it up.) Or, you can use the stress as a launching point for laughter, which will help you feel better, lower your blood pressure, ease your nerves, and restore the natural luster to your hair. (Again, I'm not positive about the last one.)

Look at it this way; when things are going wrong and bad luck seems to have made you its poster child, you can complain, get angry, throw things, and feel rotten. Or you can find the humor in the situation, laugh, smile, and know that the bad things are only temporary.

If you want to find out how to find the humor in your situation, give me a call...but not right now. The power just went out and I tripped over the dog, spilling my glass of tomato juice on the new white sofa. I guess it's going to be one of those days.

OUTLAW LAUGHTER TIP #2
You've Got To Be Kidding!

The secret to adding more laughter to your life is to recognize the funny things that surround you every day. Reading the newspaper each morning helps me achieve this goal.

As soon as I can get the newspaper...away from my dog...I open it to the comics. The funny pages are an excellent way to begin any day. If you begin the day with laughter, it makes all of the front-page news about corrupt government officials, mad cows, sick chickens, and disgruntled postal workers that much easier to handle.

After I have placed myself in a more jovial mood, I turn to the serious news of the day. Once you have gotten to a place of "comic awareness" even staid news can take on an air of frivolity. For instance, I recently saw a headline in the paper that read, *"Alligator wrestler bitten on head in stunt."* Naturally, a headline such as this captured my immediate attention.

Apparently a professional alligator wrestler (an oxymoron in itself) named Kenny Cypress wanted to enhance his alligator wrestling show for tourists by sticking HIS HEAD in an ALLIGATOR'S MOUTH. Now, I am not a professional alligator wrestler but it seems to me that sticking your head in an alligator's mouth makes about as much sense as asking the policeman who arrested you for speeding if he has a beer can opener in his squad car.

An amazing thing happened when Kenny stuffed his head into the alligator; the alligator BIT HIM! Wow, what are the odds on this? Both Kenny and the alligator survived this incident but reading this story still raised some interesting questions for me.

1) Did anybody capture this event on videotape?
2) If so, could I get a copy of it?
3) Has Kenny ever seen "When Animals Attack" on the Fox network?
4) Is there any chance that we could get Louis Farrakhan to stick his head in an alligator's mouth?

Laughter is where you find it my friends, and if you really try, you can find it anyplace you look.

OUTLAW LAUGHTER TIP #3

When The Moon Hits Your Eye Like A Big Pizza Pie, That's A Messy!

I recently visited a delightful Italian restaurant in Los Angeles, California that had a catchy, trendy name like the Pasta and Pickle, or the Cheese and Coronary but since no one is allowed to smoke within 12 miles of any California restaurant, the restaurants no longer carry any matches. Had they had matches, I would have grabbed a pack—even though I don't smoke—and that pack would have provided me with the actual name of the establishment. So, as a side note to California restaurants everywhere, even if people can't smoke, they will still steal your matches so be sure to put your name on them.

This restaurant—The Mob and Olive, I think—had mediocre food, a house wine that tasted like a mixture of Kool Aid and sweat socks, and a waiting line A BLOCK LONG! As I sat there attempting to digest my appetizer of pork rinds marinara, I tried to figure out why on earth people would stand in line for such subpar fare. Then, out of the clear night sky, it hit me like a stale roll. All of the waiters and waitresses passed out song sheets for the song 'Amore' as a recorded Dean Martin crooned the words "when the moon hits your eye like a bigga pizza pie...that's amore." All of a sudden this was more than a restaurant, it was a party.

The staff circulated to every table, toasting the patrons and singing away. Even the matre' d and the hostess made sure that they visited every diner and raised their glass in a toast of bienvenude.[3] Everybody was singing, and drinking, and swaying to the music and all of a sudden we forgot that we were eating less than spectacular food because we were HAVING FUN.

Imagine how your customers would feel if they had fun when they did business with your employees. A little

---

[3] Literally, "Batteries not included."

laughter goes a long way to overcome everyday service problems. Encourage your people to put their customers in a spirit of bienvenude and you will be amazed at the results. And just for the record, yes, I will return to that restaurant again. You can get good food anywhere, but not good fun.

Outlaw Laughter Tip #4
Laugh Or Die...You Make The Call

You can say a lot of things about laughter. You can say that it is fun to do. You can say that it's 100% natural. You can even say that it doesn't stain delicate garments. But the main thing you should say about laughter is that IT CAN KEEP YOU ALIVE.

First of all, let me state that I have absolutely no proof of anything I am about to say and any statistics are fictitious. Now that I have that disclaimer out of the way, let me proceed with my case.

We will begin with "Laughter and Heart Disease." It is a well-known fact that 4 out of 5 dentists agree that laughter exercises the heart and stimulates the blood flow. Therefore, if you don't laugh and do not have stimulated blood flow, you will die. The one exception to this rule was my Uncle Bernie who lived to 97—and was the bitterest old man in history. Who knows, had he laughed a little he might have made it to 98.

Next, let me point out that laughter will keep you from losing your hair. What do really stressed out, hyperactive, totally serious, non-laughing people do when they are distraught? They PULL THEIR HAIR OUT! Laughing people never pull their hair out but turn their energies to aerobic exercises like "grabbing their sides" or "slapping their knees."

Finally, let me just say that laughter has been documented to cause ebullience of the cervojugularfelliniary gland and I don't have to tell you how important that is to a good health program.

In closing let me say that if you laughed at anything in this chapter you will live a long time. If you didn't laugh, call my cousin Lou. He sells life insurance.

OUTLAW LAUGHTER TIP #5

Laugh All The Way To The Bank...
And The Supermarket...
And The Dry Cleaner...

How much of your day do you spend laughing? The average person—and I am not insinuating that you are average—spends less than 2 minutes a day laughing. This is considerably less time than we spend standing in line, yelling at our kids, or arguing with our co-workers. Why is it that we spend more time on activities that give us stress than we do on activities that make us feel better? *(note: this is a rhetorical question which does not require an answer and will not be counted towards your final grade)*.

When you add more laughter into your life you have a much better chance of living longer, feeling better, and not climbing a tall building with a high powered rifle.

Additionally, laughter helps to curtail one of the biggest problems in the workplace, employee absenteeism. Employees calling in to work "sick" account for over 2 billion lost man-hours per year.[4] Many times these employees are not even "sick" but just don't want to come to work. Why would anybody not want to go to work you may ask? Probably because they found something more fun to do. If employees knew that they would laugh and have fun at their job, they would show up every day.

The bottom line is this—if you want to improve your bottom line, add more laughter into your day. You will have less stress, be more productive, have more fun at your job, and you will even be nicer to your customers who will in turn give you more money. It's a simple equation,

More Punch Lines = Bigger Bottom Lines.

---

[4] This is a totally fabricated statistic but you'll have to admit that it looks pretty impressive.

OUTLAW LAUGHTER TIP #6

Take Two Punchlines And
Call Me In The Morning

Q: What has four legs and one arm?

A: A pit bull.

Did that joke make you laugh? No? Well, then, try this one.

A guy walks into a bar with his dog on a leash. When the bartender tells him that they don't allow dogs in the bar the man replies, "This is my Seeing Eye dog." The bartender allows the man and the dog to stay.

After finishing his drink, the man leaves. On his way out he meets another man with a Chihuahua on a leash. The second man said, "Hey, how did you get your dog in the bar? They don't allow dogs in that bar." The first gentleman told him, "I told the bartender it was my Seeing Eye dog."

The second man walked into the bar with his dog and sat down. The bartender immediately said, "Hey pal, no dogs in the bar." The man replied, "It's my Seeing Eye dog." Not easily fooled, the bartender said, "It's a Chihuahua!" To which the man replied, "They gave me a Chihuahua?!"

Maybe you laughed, maybe you just smiled, or maybe you have stopped reading altogether by now. The point is that if you smiled or laughed—even briefly, you helped to lower your stress level. Laughter will do that for you and it is only one of its many benefits.

Recent studies point out that 52% of American executives will die from a stress related ailment. That can include high blood pressure, heart disease, and, in many cases, alcohol and drug abuse. Experts have given us many ways to combat stress including diet, exercise, meditation, and even reruns of Gilligan's Island...also known as video morphine. Now, however, even the so-called experts are recognizing the benefits of laughter.

When you laugh, it is impossible to retain any tension in your body I am sure that at one time or another you have had to move a heavy piece of furniture. You are usually at one end of the Lazy-Boy brand recliner and your brother-in-law (we'll call him Itchy in this example) is at the other end. As the two of you are maneuvering the chair down the stairs, Itchy either, a) tells a joke, b) performs a natural bodily function in a rather loud and resounding way, or c) has his ill fitting toupee slip over his eyes. In any case, you begin to laugh. As you laugh, what is the first thing you have to do? You have to PUT DOWN THE CHAIR. You cannot hold muscle tension and laugh at the same time. As a professional comedian, I have, from time to time, had people come up to me after a show and share that they laughed so hard they almost "wet their pants." This is taking the release of muscular tension just a bit too far. The point of the matter is that laughter will help you to relieve tension, which is a major cause of stress.

So the next time you are feeling tension, apprehension, trepidation, or any of those other big words that mean stress, watch a funny movie, visit a comedy club, or read a funny publication. You don't need a prescription, you'll suffer no side effects, and you will feel your stress and tension melt away.

Study Questions For This Chapter

1. Men think the Three Stooges are funny; women think they are stupid. Discuss.

2. What is the proper action to follow the statement, "Pull my finger"?

3. Women don't find this funny either. Explain.

4. Why is it called a punch line if nobody gets punched?

5. Pauly Shore. Explain.

Dale Irvin, csp, cpae

Dale Irvin is a very funny speaker. He is also an author, actor, and widely televised comedian. But speaking is what Dale does first, foremost, and incredibly well.

In addition to 100 national TV appearances, Dale has appeared in concert with Jay Leno, Paul Anka, The Four Tops, and The Temptations.

Dale has received professional speaking's two highest awards as presented by the National Speakers Association. In 1988 Dale earned the designation of CSP, Certified Speaking Professional; and in 1995 was given the highest recognition and inducted into the CPAE Speakers Hall of Fame. Dale is one of only 67 speakers in the world to hold both of these titles.

Dale is the author of three books and publishes *Funny Business*, a monthly humor newsletter with international distribution.

Dale's programs include:

"Laughter Doesn't Hurt" This speech is more like a one-man show in which he demonstrates the healing power of laughter in such a hilarious way that the audience should be illness-free forever.

"Five Minute Funnies" Imagine having a comedy monologue presented to your audience once or twice a day based on *what has just happened!* Dale can do it, finding humor in every meeting and social function. His material is clean, intelligent, and timely. This is a one-of-a-kind presentation.

"Custom Put-On" Dale is introduced to your audience as anyone from the new vice president of sales to the junior senator from Montana. Together you decide on a character and Dale will create a program that will confuse and baffle the audience until they catch on and enjoy the fun. Dale has even performed this program in the character of a woman...and a darn good looking one at that.

"Power Thinking" This three hour creative thinking seminar delivers solid creative thinking techniques in a fun and memorable way. It is a very unique break-out session.

"Time Is On Our Side" Many people have covered the subject of time management but never in such an entertaining way. This is a half-day seminar.

"The Corporate Challenge" Dale has developed his own game show which is used to reinforce information your audience has learned during the course of the meeting. It is full of laughs and is a very fun way to learn.

Dale Irvin is a smart savvy guy with a button-down style and a way of finding humor in just about everything. He laughs at life...and life, in return, laughs with him.

For more information on Dale Irvin contact:

Just Imagine®
P. O. Box 9061
Downers Grove, IL 60515
800 951-7321
www.daleirvin.com

Up Close And Personal With Dale Irvin

Birthday: January 28.

What Year? Every year.

Birthplace: Cleveland. Ohio.

Current Home: Downers Grove, Illinois, where every day is double coupon day.

Occupation: Speaker.

Favorite Performers: Gentle Ben, JoJo the Dog Face Boy, Robert Goulet.

Favorite Pigout Food: Tapioca.

I Like To Stay Home And Watch: My neighbors; they have no draperies.

I'm Better Than Anyone Else When It Comes To: Generating static electricity.

I've Never Been Able To Figure Out: How to refold a road map.

One Thing Everyone Has Tried But Me: Long division.

Behind My Back My Friends Say: "I wish he'd turn around."

Three Words That Best Describe Me: Location, location, location.

Dale Irvin Order Form

"Laughter Doesn't Hurt" • *Dale Irvin's hilarious book based upon his popular one man show of the same name. Dale talks about the beneficial and healing powers of laughter and then provides 62 "Comedy Vitamins"–funny stories to be taken...one a day... to improve your mental outlook and realign your sense of humor. (238 pages – Paperback):* *$12.95*

"Laughter Doesn't Hurt" – THE LIVE PERFORMANCE • *Audio cassette of Dale's one-man show that inspired the book. Together, the audio cassette AND the book make the perfect gift ensemble. (audio cassette)* *$15.00*
(audio cassette AND book) *$25.00*

"Dale Irvin Rewrites History" • *Dale takes a hilarious look a real people and actual historic events with totally made up stories. (book)* *$12.95*

Dale Irvin's 50 Favorite Jokes • *Audio cassette that contains...well, 50 of Dales favorite jokes. Feel free to memorize all 50, impress people at parties, or just make strangers laugh. At $10 that's only 20¢ per joke! (audio cassette)* *$10.00*

Jokes For The New Millennium • *Dale follows up his 50 favorite jokes with 50 more of his all time favorites. (audio cassette)* *$10.00*

Funny Business • *Dale's monthly humor newsletter is now publishing in its 15th year. Funny Business features humorous observations, news stories, headlines, editorials, and others bits of humorous information no human being can live without. A full year's subscription to Funny Business (12 issues)....$36.00*

Outlaw Wisdom • *A thought provoking book of quotes by the Outlaws of Success. (book)* *$9.95*

The Outlaws Of Success • *Bending the rules without crossing the line by the Outlaws of Success. (book)* *$12.95*

Please include $3.00 for shipping and handling.
Please pay by check or money order.

For more information contact:
Just Imagine®
P. O. Box 9061 • Downers Grove, IL 60515
800- 951-7321

CHAPTER 3

THE STEPS TO MAKE
YOUR OWN RULES

■■■■■■■■■■■■■■■■■■■■■

by Scott McKain, CSP, CPAE

THE STEPS TO MAKE YOUR OWN RULES

by Scott McKain, CSP, CPAE

■ ■ ■ ■ ■ ■ ■ ■ ■ ■ ■ ■ ■ ■ ■ ■ ■ ■ ■ ■

The Older I Get, The Smarter My Father Becomes.

C ertainly, Dad continues to say some pretty intelligent things—however, what I am referring to is how ingenious some of the laws I dismissed in my youth appear to me now.

> **Dad once said to me, "Rules are not made to be broken— only bent when it is appropriate."**

That is what this chapter—and this book—is really all about.

In my first book, *Just Say Yes!* I examined some of the rules that parents give to children: "Don't cross the street without looking both ways!" "Don't chew with your mouth open!" "Don't leave the house without clean underwear on—you might be in an accident!" Let's face it, those are pretty important rules that we should not bend. Crossing streets safely, eating properly and undergarment hygiene are all important for all of us. My problem is that those rules presented to us early in life were all stated in a negative—rather than positive—fashion. In other words, we were taught what we should NOT do, instead of what we should.

A Different Approach...

Let's take a different approach for this book—some of the rules we were given as children, and are ingrained into our thinking, are totally *wrong* for application in our adult lives. Our problem is that we have not erased them from our "mental tapes" so they continue to play over and over in our heads and have a hold on our subconscious thoughts. Here is an example: "Don't talk to strangers." Obviously, we do not want our kids out talking to people they do not know. However, many of the pleasures and enrichments of our personal and professional lives as adults come from the new people we meet.

If we follow the adage of "don't talk to strangers," we will miss much of the happiness of life. We will not grow intellectually or emotionally to the degree we want. If you are a sales professional, try making a "cold call" on someone who really believes they should not "talk to strangers." If you want to be a true "Outlaw of Success" you should find situations where you can talk to strangers—and learn from them!

Often the rules we learned as children are contradictory. How do we resolve the conflict between "Children should be seen and not heard" with "The squeaky wheel gets the grease"? My suggestion is that we follow the Outlaw principle: *Bend the rules without crossing the line.*

As adults, we need to understand that "squeaky wheels" are often just an irritant. They may get an occasional "greasing"—but as often as not, they do not receive the attention they desire because they have been so obnoxious that people go out of their way to avoid them! If you decide to be a "squeaky wheel," do it very selectively.

I once had a coach that was always screaming and hollering at his players. He would not let a single play go by on the basketball court without becoming very vocal about how we had failed to perform up to his expectations. Every practice and every game was a time for him to attempt to attain a higher level of vocal volume. Guess what happened?

One of our best players quit the team. The rest of us merely "tuned out" the coach. When a time came that we should have been yelled at, his screaming had no impact. We could not determine what was important and what was not because of his constant histrionics. Do colleagues and family members tune you out because you are nothing but a "squeaky wheel?"

Wait a minute, though—we were also taught as kids that we should be "seen and not heard." As life progressed for us, however, we learned that there were times we had to speak up—or else we would be left behind.

The Past *May Not Be* Prologue

What I am suggesting here is that we have learned through the experiences we have had in life that the rules we were taught and were ingrained in our behavior had relevance for a particular time. It does not mean, however, that the rules we learned in our youth should apply in every situation today.

Would you try to show up on a gridiron and look at the goal posts—then hold up a basketball and say, "Don't take more than two steps without dribbling or else it is called 'travelling'?" Of course not. The rules of basketball do not apply on a field of grass with yardage markers. Yet, too many of us try to make old rules apply to the situations of today.

Outlaws of Success understand that you have to **create** rules that fit the following standards:

1. Your morals and ethics
2. The law of the land
3. The demands placed upon you by yourself and others
4. The situation in which you find yourself
5. What just feels "right" to you

1) Your morals and ethics

In this time of great debate about what we should know about the private lives of public figures and what the values of the nation are, the more significant questions are: What are your ethics? What will you stand for? What **won't** you stand for?

An Outlaw of Success may break the rules that have been prescribed by a cultural norm, but we never cross the line in regards to our own moral code. If you live in a manner that is incongruous with your values, you won't find success, anyway.

I believe, however, that the problem for most of us is not living apart from our moral code, rather it is living day-to-day with no development of any kind of personal ethical standard. The musician I grew up with in southern Indiana, John Mellencamp, once sang that if you "don't stand for something you'll fall for anything." I think that is true! By being unwilling do be introspective enough to develop our own personal moral code—or by just being too damn lazy to do so—we end up succumbing to those who have a stronger will. A troubled mind and heart prevents success from happening. True stress is generated not when others disapprove of what you do—it is when you object to your own actions.

2) The law of the land

I would never want you to think that you should not obey the law. Our civilization is based upon the fact that we have laws that are quite important for upholding life in an orderly society. The law of the land should be one—and a very important—aspect of consideration.

However, any good Outlaw knows that laws can sometimes be well intentioned and end up just plain silly. We have all seen the many articles written on antiquated laws in many cities and states. You know the kind—one town has a law saying you can't walk your dog during a full moon. One state had a law that remained on the books for decades that women couldn't be seen in public wearing pants after a certain time of day…another says that men who do not remove their hat in a theatre will be arrested. (Hey, maybe that last one isn't all bad!)

The point here is that even laws have degrees of legitimacy. Do not let yourself become bound by laws— real or implied—that are irrelevant.

3) The demands placed upon you by yourself and others

Most people would tell you that the demands that others place upon you are not of importance. What really matters, these people will proclaim, are the demands you choose to place upon yourself.

Well, as an Outlaw, I must disagree.

The demands a baby places upon his or her parents for support can not—and should never—be ignored. The demands placed upon us by society to be good citizens contribute to the welfare of the community. What other people want, expect and demand from us can be a very positive factor when kept in its proper perspective.

You are the ultimate judge on the relevance of the expectations that others may have about you. I believe that real maturity as a human being is in the ability to ascertain whether someone's expectations about you are generated from a positive or negative motive.

The most important demands, however, are the ones you place upon yourself. Have you ever been exercising alone and the thought pops into your head, "I think

I won't do the second set of reps." Maybe you tell yourself you can cut your morning run a little short because no one will ever know.

The problem, of course, is that YOU will know. The lowering of expectations precedes the loss of discipline and both are disastrous to success. Keep your personal expectations high and you will be amazed at the success you achieve.

4) The situation in which you find yourself

Sometimes we just have to hold on and make it through a difficult circumstance. Other times, it seems as if we are "bulletproof" and nothing we can do is wrong. (For some strange reason, life seems to have more of the former than the latter.)

There have been many books lately about "situational" living. From "Situational Ethics" to "Situational Leadership," much thought has been given about how the situation often determines the response. What I want to ask is, "Do you think this is new?" Any parent knows that the rules for your eight-year-old are different from a son or daughter of eighteen. To be a true "Outlaw of Success" you must design a strategy for improving your life *based upon the situation in which you are currently living.*

I am so tired of motivational speakers who ignore the fact that some people are facing really difficult predicaments. Whether it is stress from the loss of a job in a corporate merger, or the anguish of divorce, if you are facing tough times, the best advice anyone can give you is to deal with it—from where you are right now. You have heard the old cliché about the "journey of a thousand miles begins with a single step." The part I would add is that that step must begin somewhere. The best place is where you are standing right now.

Don't make your planning for success merely "pie in the sky." Be realistic. Remember what the wise man once said, "Unrealistic goals do not motivate—they merely frustrate."

5) What just feels "right" to you

Women tend to call it "intuition." Many men talk about their "gut feel." Either way, I think they both describe the same phenomenon. Most of the time, we know what we should and should not be doing.

In the Old West, the gunslingers would often hide out if they did not have good feelings about a particular day. Rather than be challenged to a duel on a day they didn't feel confident, they would simply lay low. No cowboy could tolerate being called a "chicken" (or worse!), so if your perceptivity told you it was not a good day, it was easier and more acceptable to just disappear than risk defeat or death.

Today's business world often does not afford us the luxury of "hiding out." (Although you may have a favorite spot in your office to make a good attempt to do so!) This means that we have to pay special attention to how we "feel" about the decisions we make and the people with whom we associate. Some anthropologists believe that this intuition is part of the human genetic makeup. In his book, "The Gift of Fear," author and violence expert Gavin De Becker discusses this assertion. The cavemen and cavewomen who listened to their intuition were the ones who lived and passed that genetic code to their descendents. We, on the other hand, are so protected by technology that we are safe in spite of ourselves. Safe, however, does not mean successful. To be a true "Outlaw of Success" you understand that knowledge and theories are important—but it is just as vital that you follow your heart and do what "feels right" as well.

One More Point and I'm Through!

(That's what my 300-pound grandfather used to say going through a barbed-wire fence. It's also true of this chapter!)

This success stuff has GOT to be fun for you or else it will not happen. You may sense a theme here with all of the "Outlaws" —we are serious about the fact that you have to have fun! Humor is your balance-pole on the tightrope of life. Use it liberally as a tool to keep your batteries charged and your spirits lifted—and to pave the potholes you will encounter on your bumpy road to success! Go get 'em, Outlaw!

WANTED

6'0"

5'6"

5'0"

SCOTT MCKAIN

Scott McKain, CSP, CPAE

Scott McKain has been a professional speaker, author, seminar leader and broadcast journalist for more than 20 years. He has entertained, educated and inspired corporate and association audiences in 49 states and 13 countries.

His programs blend research into today's successful business leaders with media interviews of top celebrities, in order to present up-to-the-minute information to inspire and educate his audiences. For more than twelve years, over two million people watched him every week on television as a journalist and commentator.

Scott is a recipient of the **Council of Peers Award of Excellence**, considered to be the "Oscar"™ of the professional speaking industry. He is a member of the **Professional Speaker's "Hall of Fame,"** an honor that has been presented to about one hundred of the top communicators in the world—Ronald Reagan, Zig Ziglar and Norman Vincent Peale to name a few.

He is also a **Certified Speaking Professional**—the highest earned designation in professional speaking and is one of the youngest members elected to the **Speakers Roundtable**—a select group of outstanding business speakers considered by many to be the best in the world.

Scott has served on the Board of Directors of the National Safety Council, the Advisory Council on Vocational Education and was Chairman of the official Bicentennial project for his home state of Indiana. He has been named to **"Who's Who Among America's Emerging Leaders,"** and as one of the **"Outstanding Young Men in America."**

Among Scott's many speaking appearances over the years, was his selection by Arnold Schwarzenegger to be emcee and speaker on the White House lawn for the **"Great American Workout."** He has also interviewed some of the nation's top celebrities on the essence and secrets of success—people like Tom Hanks, Meryl Streep, Bruce Willis and Jim Carrey.

Scott is president of the McKain Performance Group, based in Del Mar, California; a company dedicated to improving personal and professional performance and is currently working in his latest book, **"ALL Business is Show Business!"™**

Scott McKain Order Form

Just Say YES! A Step Up To Success! • *The seven cassette, fourteen day program to personal achievement that started it all! As seen on national TV!!! Learn the importance of values and priorities, goal setting and communication, and the "Six Steps Up To Success!" Sold on national television for $79.95 ...special price for Outlaw Wisdom readers:* *$49.95*

Just Say YES! A Step up To Success • *The hot-selling book based on the audio cassette album. With a foreword by baseball hall of famer, Jim Palmer! A must read!!! In bookstores for $29.95...special Outlaw Wisdom price:* *$19.95*

Just Say YES! A Step Up To Success! • *A full-hour video of the best of the entertainment and enlightenment of Scott McKain. (VHS format only)* *$19.95*

Dragonslayers! • *Scott's first audio program. Recorded live and in-studio. The cassettes of humor and information on change, humor and relationships. (Limited quantities available.)....$19.95*

Single audio tape of fun with Scott! *Laugh and learn. Some of the best of Scott's classic humor and some new fun with a master of message and merriment!* *$10.00*

Outlaw Wisdom • *A book of quotes by the Outlaws of Success.* *$9.95*

The Outlaws Of Success • *A book about bending the rules without crossing the line by the Outlaws of Success.* ..*$12.95*

SAVE!!! get the whole package for only $99.95

Visa, Master Card, and American Express accepted.
Please include $4.50 for shipping and handling.

For more information contact:
McKain Performance Group
P. O. Box 5000, #400
Del Mar, CA 92014
800-297-5844
www.scottmckain.com

CHAPTER 4

WANTED:
SUCCESSFUL OUTLAWS

■ ■

by Mark Sanborn, CSP, CPAE

WANTED:
SUCCESSFUL OUTLAWS

by Mark Sanborn, CSP, CPAE

■■■■■■■■■■■■■■■■■■■■■■

In the days of the old west, outlaws earned their infamous reputations because of their relentless disregard for the law and their renegade natures. But even the wildest among them usually lived by a code of conduct. They didn't think twice about breaking laws that didn't suit them, but they did abide by their own standards. Who said there was no honor among thieves? To survive, they developed rules of behavior that kept them out of trouble and away from the stockade. These internal laws served as a sort of personal compass for the outlaw. We each need a personal compass by which to navigate.

Try navigating your way to success with nothing to guide you. You will be pinned on the valley floor surrounded by a ridge of rules that will keep you holed up in the middle of nowhere. The truth is, success has very few rules but many laws. Almost all rules are based on averages: if, on average, something works for most people, it becomes a rule. The natural evolution of that rule is that if you follow the rules, you'll probably end up being average. That is not exactly a blueprint for pulling off a big heist!

Outlaws of success make their own rules. They aren't interested in what works for everybody else— they care about finding what works for themselves.

For example, I've often heard that the rule of successful selling is to talk about price last. Get the potential customer sold on all the benefits of the product and theoretically, the price barrier drops to midget height. Well, my theory is completely different. I like to talk price as early as possible so that there aren't any surprises. I don't want time wasted trying to sell a client who can't afford my fee. That's why we quote fees right up front. I've become successful, in part, by breaking an accepted "rule" of selling.

But laws are different than rules. First of all, laws are above individual preference or choice. The laws of success aren't the arbitrary creation of a single person or group of people; they are based on higher universal axioms. The laws of success are external principles that are constant across time and circumstance. An example: you reap what you sow. Just as you can't get carrots if you've sown corn, you can't achieve harmonious relationships by creating conflict. It doesn't matter who you are or what you do, the law applies.

I believe in bending—and even breaking—the rules without crossing the line. The line, for me, is doing what's right. There is no right way to do the wrong thing. That's the law of morality. Becoming an outlaw of success won't get you into any legal or moral difficulty. On the contrary, it will clarify your personal moral compass and assist you in doing the right thing regardless of whether anybody but yourself is watching.

When it comes to success, many rules were created by others that are not helpful in that quest. There are plenty of rules that have been created that are not for my benefit—or yours. Those are the rules I love to bend and sometimes break. The rules are so stifling that I feel called to put on my black hat and let a posse try to catch me as I break the constraints that could make me average, if I allowed it.

The rule of conformity says blend in, look alike. The law of uniqueness shouts stand out, celebrate diversity. The rule of weirdness says attract attention any way you can. The law of recognition says that "if you've done it, it ain't braggin'." With a little practice and thought you'll start to recognize the difference between rules and laws, and in the process you'll know which to keep and which to bend or break.

There are 5 laws that every outlaw of success must follow to break out of the rules that keep law-abiding businesspeople clustered in mediocrity like herd of a cattle moving across the range. Keep these laws and you could find your name alongside some of the most prestigious outlaws of history—Ben Franklin, Lee Iaccoca, Sally Ride, Ghandi, Susan B. Anthony, Martin Luther King, Jr. and you! Break these laws and you lose the right to be a successful maverick riding confidently toward your aspirations. No jail time—just middle-of-the-road conformity and average results. Here they are:

1. The Law of Passion
2. The Law of Opportunity
3. The Law of Effectiveness
4. The Law of Follow-through
5. The Law of Persistence

The Law of Passion

Not so long ago, after two years of deliberation, negotiation and angst, I bought a Harley Davidson motorcycle. I'd ridden dirt bikes growing up and street bikes through my college years, but it had been 15 years since I'd owned a bike. I figured, why not buy the very best? It's a custom built '91 softtail, and if that doesn't mean much to you, just trust me—it's sweet. Even people who normally have no particular interest in motorcycles or things mechanical have approached to me tell me what a beautiful machine it is.

Before taking the plunge, I had been reading about Harleys, going to Harley shows and generally noticing every Harley that crossed my path. I decided that I was either going to get my own or stop looking at them and reading about them. I got tired of living vicariously. It had been a fairly long time since I indulged myself with a major discretionary purchase ("discretionary" sounds better than "frivolous"). But most importantly, buying the Harley was good for my soul. And the soul is the source of passion. Let me explain.

Perhaps you're familiar with the Harley Davidson story about how America's last motorcycle manufacturer had lost its way. The Japanese began their assault on the American motorcycle market in 1959 with small displacement motorcycles with electric starters, an attractive alternative to the big V-Twin hogs.

By the mid-'70s, Japan was producing big displacement bikes to compete head to head with Harley Davidson; their overall share of market plummeted. To make matter worse, Harleys had developed a reputation for incredibly poor quality. 50-60% of the bikes rolling off the production line failed to pass inspection. The company's existence was threatened.

In 1981, 13 of the company's executives bought the company back from AMF and began a spectacular turnaround. Hourly employees were provided extensive and sophisticated training, given increased authority and involved in the manufacturing process; in short, they were empowered before the word became fashionable in business circles. Employees started building world-class motorcycles and revived the ailing company. It wasn't just a turn-around, it was more like a revival.

Today it can be tough to buy a new Harley Davidson. Call a HD dealership and—if you're lucky—they'll put you on a waiting list in case one of the customers who has already made a deposit—without even knowing what color and sometimes not even which model Harley they'll get—doesn't qualify for financing.

If you talk to someone who owns and rides a Harley, you might get a glimpse into the collective psyche of the Harley brotherhood and, yes, sisterhood (It isn't unusual for spouses to each ride their own hog). People are crazy about their Harleys. Personally, I am a certified Harley fanatic. Some of the more well-known past and present Harley aficionados are Malcolm Forbes, Clark Gable, Kyle Petty, Jay Leno, Arnold Schwarrzenegger and even Elvis (and who knows? He may still be riding....).

That story ought to move you at least a little bit. Harley Davidson, the come-back-kid, the Cinderella story—down but not defeated. The company has become a symbol of quality and the American Dream reclaimed. When you buy their products, you buy a piece of the story. But there's something more to it than just a great comeback story of American pride and Yankee ingenuity. Beau Allen Pacheco, a journalist at Big Twin magazine, captured my sentiments when he wrote:

> As I see it, life comes down to choosing which of two philosophies you're going to follow. Philosophy #1 was stated clearly in the seminal book Catch 22 by the character Dunbar when he said, "Life is longer if it's filled with boredom and discomfort..."
>
> Philosophy #2 was stated with equal clarity by the author Tom Robbins when he wrote, "These things can enlarge the soul: Laughter, danger, imagination, meditation, wild nature, passion, compassion, beauty, iconoclasm, and driving around in the rain with the top down..."

When I stood there with my hands in my pockets considering the purchase of my very first Harley, gazing down at the chrome, trying to justify the money against the rewards, I was actually weighing #1 against #2. Long life vs. enlarging the soul.

I'm very glad that I opted for #2. Personally, I like the idea of enlarging the soul and a long life. Pacheco is right on the money—we can opt for long, ordinary and uncomfortable or we can choose to enlarge the soul and channel passions.

Which philosophy are you living?

You can operate out of your head, and people may call you an intellectual—that's Philosophy #1. You can operate out of your heart, and you'll be described as sensitive and emotional. But when you operate out of passion—philosophy #2—you will probably become known as a success.

Intellect without emotion is sterile; emotion without intellect is irrational. One way to describe passion is to call it the synergy of intellect and emotion, of head and heart. In synergy, the output is greater than the sum of the individual parts. And passion is a primary product of the soul.

(Let me add here that I am speaking of soul in a secular sense, not because the theological soul is not important, but because I don't choose to tackle that issue in this chapter.)

The world and the workplace can easily diminish our passion. The demands, uncertainty, stress, worry and litany of problems makes it easy to retreat into our heads rather than live out of our hearts. The danger is that we remain intellectual or sensitive, but lose our passion for our careers and our lives. And when that has happened, we've decreased rather than enlarged our souls.

Ray Bradbury has lead an incredibly rich life and influenced thousands through his books, screenplays and other creative endeavors. He has, in my appraisal, lived life with soul. He describes his experience like this:

"That is the kind of life I've had. Drunk, and in charge of a bicycle, as an Irish police report once put it. Drunk with life, that is, and not knowing where off to next. And the trip? Exactly one half terror, exactly one half enthusiasm."

How many of us are living our lives so cautiously and carefully that our primary accomplishment will be only to arrive safely at death?

The law of passion says if you pursue those things you aren't passionate about, you will seldom achieve spectacular success. And if you do achieve success in areas of your life where you lack passion, you won't enjoy it very much. You will be most successful in those endeavors where you are passionate, and pursuing those activities and experiences will be good for your soul.

Follow your passion.

The Law of Opportunity

The phone is ringing—again; there's yet another meeting to attend (it started five minutes ago); someone at the door needs your attention right now, and your pager is going off. Your blood pressure is rising almost as quickly as the number of messages in your e-mail inbox.

When you finally answer the phone on the tenth ring, your tone of voice gives you away. The caller feels guilty for having called at an obviously bad time. Then when you turn to the person at the door, your abrupt greeting sends him scurrying away mumbling an apology. Finally, when you take your seat at the meeting, your energy level is on empty, and your attention wanders as important issues are discussed.

Later that night, after dinner, you find you have little time—and even less enthusiasm—to give to your kids. You think, "Maybe if I get a couple of hours of work in before bed, I'll be caught up for tomorrow...."

And when you finally turn the light off at a quarter to one, you wonder why the success you've worked so hard to achieve doesn't make you feel, well— successful. As you lie there, you think about the not-so-long-ago days when you weren't invited to high-powered meetings, the phone rang less frequently, and you weren't the first person others came to for advice. You wasted no time in climbing the ladder—so why aren't you enjoying your success? Why is it that you—and the people around you—are actually suffering from it?

More often than not, success can feel as emotionally draining as a gun fight at the O.K. Corral. In today's workplace people are having to work harder to get more done with fewer resources. And for many, it just isn't any fun—we're busy making money, but in the process, we're sacrificing joy and a sense of meaning.

I know how it happens. Several years ago, I too was close to premature flame-out. Most people would say that my problems were good ones to have. My business was so brisk that it was hard to keep up, my involvement as a board member of a national association offered me many new responsibilities and challenges, and I was traveling nearly non-stop. However, as glamorous as that lifestyle sounds, I wasn't having much fun living it, and I found it increasingly difficult to give people the attention and consideration they deserved. When the phone rang, I didn't want to answer it. I wanted to smash it. I wasn't carrying the weight of the world on my shoulders, but it did feel like a small planet.

I knew that soon I would be experiencing the repercussions of others' frustration with me. (When you aren't having much fun, rest assured that neither are your clients, colleagues, friends, or family!) I wondered, "How can anyone live happily and lead effectively with so many oppressive obligations?"

When I finally stopped my frenetic pace long enough to slow down and look for an answer, I took a step back and reviewed everything I had learned from studying and working with effective leaders. I pondered all that I had read about the lives of great people. And suddenly,

I was struck with an insight—the people who change the world—their companies, communities, and families—rarely act from a sense of oppressive obligation. In fact, the people we call "true leaders" almost always act from a sense of incredible opportunity. They don't change the world because they have to—they change the world because they want to—they are filled with passion and see life as opportunity!

I doubt that Mother Teresa woke up even one morning and complained, "Oh, Lord, not more lepers!" She did some of the hardest work on the planet, and she seemed to have more fun than we who sit in plush, air-conditioned offices. How can that be?

It's a matter of perspective. When we feel harried and pressured, we tend to look at our circumstances as oppressive obligations. On the other hand, those few who live happily and lead effectively view such circumstances as incredible opportunities. To put it simply: Leaders frame their lives differently.

When I learned from the example of the world's great leaders and reframed my work and life, things immediately turned around. I began to see circumstances as opportunities rather than obligations, and it has made all the difference. When the phone rings now, I respond differently. I view each call as an opportunity to serve, earn, influence, network, learn, encourage, or teach. The difference isn't in the caller or the purpose for the call; the difference is in my response.

There isn't much I absolutely have to do in life. Sure, I have a commitment to provide for my wife and son, but I could still meet that commitment if I greatly reduced my current workload or even changed careers. My colleague, Ian Percy, has often said that his family doesn't really want all the money and trappings of affluence. They would gladly live in a trailer-as long as they had him, his time, and attention. I'm sure most families would echo that sentiment.

Even in the worst circumstance, lies an opportunity. That cliché about every cloud having a silver lining really is true. As you read this, perhaps you're facing dire circumstances. Foreclosure may threaten, a primary relationship may be on the brink of disaster, or you may be fighting a serious health challenge. There is no denying that tragedy and heartbreak are real and are awful. Those life-threatening and earth shaking obstacles that knock us flat are serious and painful times. They are also opportunities. I don't say this lightly. I don't negate the tough issues that some people have to face.

Within those excruciating times is the opportunity to overcome, to save, to improve. I know many highly successful individuals who have faced terrible situations. But meeting the challenge to overcome and learn from these situations has, without fail, greatly enriched their lives. In their darkest hour, they saw and pursued that faint glimmer of light called opportunity.

To remind myself of this important life principle, I keep a sticky note over my desk. On it are three words: "Obligation or Opportunity." That simple sentiment represents one of the most important choices I make every day, every hour. Like you, I want to make a positive impact the world around me. I want to add to the lives of others, not just pass by them unnoticed. I want to be confident that my efforts do more than earn a living, that they help create a better life for myself, my family, and the clients I serve. And now I realize that the chance to accomplish this goal is not an obligation, but the greatest opportunity of all.

The Law of Effectiveness

Benjamin Disraeli said, "He who gains time gains everything." There is a common challenge facing the average person today; even though we are doing more, we are accomplishing less. Many times we feel busy, yet ineffective. We're going faster and faster accomplishing less and less. This is the law of ineffectiveness.

Why work to break the law of ineffectiveness? Why worry about being more effective and productive?

First, we need to increase our productivity so that ultimately, we can have more time to spend with the people who really matter to us. Second, the better we get at managing our time and increasing our results, the more time we have to do the things that we really enjoy doing. Our challenge is not to put more time in our lives, but to put more life in our time. Here's how the outlaws of success do it:

a. Create a plan! In the mid-1940's, a 15-year-old boy sat down to make out a list of his life's goals. He wrote down 127 goals. He wanted to explore the Congo, Nile, and Amazon rivers. He wanted to read the complete works of Shakespeare, Aristotle, and Socrates. He also decided that he would climb Mt. Everest and Mt. Kilimanjaro. He planned to take off from and land on the deck of an aircraft carrier. His final goal was to walk on the moon.

By 1986, John Goddard had accomplished 108 of those 127 goals—last I heard, John was still working on completing his list. He knows that the key to a fulfilling and successful life is having a sense of purpose and a clearly identified set of goals.

Research suggests that very few people ever take time to do what Goddard did as a 15-year-old. We don't have a sense of what we're trying to accomplish on a monthly or yearly basis. The first step in getting more done and producing results in our personal and professional lives is committing to a long-range plan of action that very carefully details the things that we want to accomplish.

b. Plan for every week. Most people say they have a daily plan, but not a weekly plan. I call this "knee-jerk time management." On Monday morning you get to the office and you have 127 things to do that week. You set out to do all 127 on Monday. By the end of the day, when the dust is settled, the list is up to 128. Not only have you not accomplished most of what you tried to do, but some things have come up during the day that you've had to add to your list.

Tuesday morning you start—full speed—to accomplish the list. And by noon on Tuesday you're so frustrated with your lack of results that you wad that list up into a ball and throw the paper out the window.

Planning one week at a time gives you a greater sense of organization and focus because it lets you control your schedule rather than letting your schedule control you.

c. Prioritize everything. Have you noticed that at the end of a typical day you've accomplished everything except the most important item on the list? This is "reversed prioritization." The easy things get done and the important things stay undone. Having a daily list is only part of the equation. Prioritizing every item on the list so that you know what needs to be done first is the next key.

d. Understand the difference between perfectionism and excellence. Many people take pride in having extremely high standards but there is a difference between having high standards and being a perfectionist. A perfectionist is someone who has a neurotic attention to details, usually stemming from insecurity. That is not excellence. Excellence is a commitment to high standards that means additional time or energy invested in a task will be noticeably better to the end-user.

Thomas Edison once said, "I don't want to invent anything that nobody wants to buy." You don't want to be guilty of spending time on a project or a product or a service if it doesn't make that product or project or service noticeably better to the end-user. You need to involve the customer in defining quality, whether that customer is a co-worker, boss, or employee.

Many of us had parents who used to say that everything worth doing is worth doing well. Mom and Dad had good intentions but they were telling a half-truth. Some things are worth doing and getting done. Some things are worth doing well. Other things are worth doing very, very well. Perfectionism is the inability to know the difference.

e. Develop discipline. Discipline is doing what needs to be done rather than doing what you want to do. It is the ability to delay immediate gratification in order to obtain long-term gratification. It isn't enough to know what needs to be done, you need the drive and the follow-through to get it done.

I believe an outlaw of success should do at least one thing every day that is difficult or unpleasant as a way of developing discipline. Furthermore, I believe in doing at least one thing a day just for the sheer fun of it, as a way of maintaining spontaneity.

f. Team up with others. The key is not doing it all yourself. Surround yourself with other like-minded outlaws. The key is to be able to communicate and get commitment from others to live up to the same high standards that you have. Trying to do it all yourself will severally limit how much you can accomplish both personally and organizationally.

There are only three real resources in the world. The average American will say their scarcest resource is money but money is really a by-product of how you invest your time and energy. The scarcest resource in our life is time. The second scarcest resource is energy. And if you invest your time and energy wisely, you can accomplish anything that you want to accomplish, including financial goals and objectives that you've set for yourself. The third resource is the time and energy of other people. If you're only good at managing your own time and energy, you're only getting two out of three. You must develop the ability to get results with people.

Even outlaws in the Wild West worked together for mutual gain. Likewise, your skill at getting results depends on how highly developed your people skills have become.

The Law of Follow-Through

A vendor tells a client he'll send him an embroidered polo shirt the client admired. It never arrives. A prospective customer asks the account executive to call back next Wednesday to discuss a potential order. The call never comes. At a dinner party, a friend promises to send a copy of an article to someone she just met. The article never gets copied, much less mailed.

Consider in the past two weeks, how many organizations or individuals have told you that there were going to do something...and then didn't do it? Consider also—what have you told others you'd do for them...that never got done?

I don't know if follow-through was better or worse in the past. It doesn't really matter, because it seems abysmal today. The mark of a professional in any field is that they always deliver what they promise. When they commit, it happens.

I have a friend who is a successful entrepreneur who created a $75 million business. When we talk, whether it's of a business or personal nature, he makes a note of what he says he's going to do. And like clockwork, he follows through. I remark that I'd like to read an article that he mentioned, and it arrives in the mail two days later.

The concept of follow-through is simple, but it is a critical skill for living and doing business on the leading edge. Follow-through is both a philosophy and a practice. Doing or not doing what we promise is a matter of integrity. Our reputations are not as good as our words, but our deeds. Inconsistency between what we say and do is lethal to integrity.

The practice is straightforward. It requires a system of recording, dating and checking on commitments. One of the primary reasons why people don't follow-through is that they just forget. They wanted to make good on their promise, but it "slipped their minds." Because so many people fail to follow through with their commitments, those that do so really get noticed. A short pencil is infinitely better than a long memory.

Since adding value is always a priority, why not get creative and follow-through with a little more than you promised? In addition to my newsletter, I have article reprints we keep on file. When I promise to send someone my business card (I'd rather send it than just hand it to them because it makes more of an impact), I include a copy of my most recent newsletter or an article reprint along with the card.

And what about personal follow-through? How many commitments do you make to yourself that aren't kept? The Novotel New York, a hotel in midtown Manhattan, surveyed guests about their preferences. 71% of those surveyed said that gym facilities are important in deciding where they stay...but only 16% said they are likely to workout during their free time!

Recently I found a book in a friend's library that looked good but was out of print. I asked my assistant to help me find a copy at a used bookstore. She did and I bought it for $5.00 (a real steal). The book is titled "Attaining Personal Greatness" by Melanie Brown. It's a 300 page book, but here's the interesting part: whoever had owned the book previously had done extensive highlighting and note taking in the margins—but only to page 69! Evidently, their quest for personal greatness had faded less than 1/4 through the book. Mark: I'd delete this whole paragraph. The lack of highlighting does not *necessarily* indicate that the quest for greatness was abandoned, even if the book *appeared* to be abandoned.

Our interests, it seems, are not always our commitments. And our commitments aren't always followed through.

How can we increase our follow-through IQ (implementation quotient)? First, consider the difference between an interest and a commitment. An interest suggests that you would enjoy or benefit from taking further action, but haven't actually decided to do so. A commitment is a decision to act.

To make more room for the real commitments in your life, learn not to let your interests distract you. Be clear about what your commitments are! Tim Redmond captured this concept when he said, "There are many things that will catch my eye, but there are only a very few that catch my heart...it is those I consider to pursue."

Next, evaluate the feasibility of your commitments. Have you made too many? Are they realistic in terms of your time, financial and skill resources? Trying to follow-through on too much results in accomplishing too little. Finally, learn to move commitments from the "expedient" category to the "essential"category.

I completed an interesting experiment during the first quarter of 1994. I was traveling nearly non-stop giving speeches and seminars. Sandwiched between engagements was a three day period of time to be spent in the studio recording a new video series on mastering change. Professionally, things couldn't have been any busier.

I had always regretted that during these periods, I would often go several days without any exercise. Travel had always disrupted my workouts, whether in the gym or on the running track. The reason, of course, was that although I fancied myself committed to exercise, I usually treated it as expedient. I did it when I could.

I decided to make exercise essential. My plan was to exercise every day—get some form of physical activity—every day for that busy 45-day period. It might mean getting up very early or working out much later than I preferred, but if that's what it took, so be it. After all, that's what needs to be done when something is essential.

Here's what happened: I achieved my goal. For 45 consecutive days I exercised every day. Some days the exercise was lighter than others. It ranged from an hour of lifting weights to running for 20 minutes and everything between. It was challenging, but I proved it was possible. Here's the catch: to make good on my personal commitment, I had to make fulfillment essential. Expedient is good for interests; essential is necessary for commitments.

Do you have a daily list where you can record the commitments you make? Do you routinely check to make sure that those commitments you record actually get accomplished in a timely manner? Do you add value to your follow-through?

Have you learned the difference between interest and commitments? Have you become over committed because you were unrealistic about the commitments you made? Have you harnessed the power of making commitments essential rather than just expedient?

To be an outlaw of success, your follow-through on commitments needs to be 100%.

The Law of Persistence

I learned the power of persistence at a very young age. I grew up on a farm in rural northeast Ohio. I was active in a youth organization called 4-H. My club needed a representative in the Safety Speaking Contest. The objective was to prepare and present a 3-5 minute speech on an area of safety. I was a good student, so I figured, "How hard can that be?" I entered my first speech contest at the age of 10. My topic was "Hunting Knife Safety" (after all, every red-blooded farm boy had a hunting knife). It was a disaster.

I did poorly, was beaten badly and was completely humiliated. I did the only reasonable thing: I determined to try again the following year. I really believe that if I had done better—if my first speech had gone pretty well—I wouldn't have been challenged to try it again. Thank heavens for abysmal failure!

The next year I won the contest. That qualified me to go on in competition. I went all the way to the state level. That's when I got beaten again. I did the only reasonable thing: I determined to keep trying until I won the state contest.

I'll spare you the details. I never won the state 4-H Safety Speaking Contest. But there were lots of other state competitions I never won. I entered every speech competition I could find and qualified for the state finals in most of them.....but never won any of them.

My final year of eligibility in speaking competition was the Future Farmers of America (today simply called FFA) Prepared Speaking Contest. The year before I was one of two state finalists. I had spoken before an audience of 1500. It seems like everyone thought I had won, except the judges. I finished second. So here I was, back for the final attempt. I was 18 years old. Nearly a decade of trying to achieve one simple goal: to win a state competition.

I did that year. And then I went to Tri-State competition and won there. Qualified for the Regional competition. Won that. And in 1976, I won the National FFA Public Speaking Contest. I had gotten so interested in public speaking that the same year, someone offered to pay me to speak. I made $150 speaking for a high school commencement. I worked my way through college doing after-dinner speeches.

Fast forward the tape. Today I am 40 years old and have been speaking professionally for over a decade. I average 90-100 speeches per year. Professional speaking is not only how I make my living, it is personally fulfilling and is some of the most fun I have.

Most people would have given up after their first speech, especially if it went as bad as mine did. And most people would have advised me to give up trying to win a state speech contest after several years of trying. But that's where outlaw thinking comes in. An outlaw of success knows that most advice doesn't apply to him or her. They break the law of mediocrity by keeping the law of persistence.

Today, I have a successful career as a professional speaker because I failed many times, but kept trying anyhow. The law of persistence paid off.

An Outlaw's Legacy

It only makes sense that when you combine passion and opportunity with effectiveness, follow-through and persistence, you create a synergy among those elements that catapults you into a higher level of success. Get bold and start thinking like an outlaw of success Say good-bye to the ordinary, to the average and to the mundane. Career stalls and average results are for those regular folks who haven't become outlaws. Of course, these five laws aren't the only laws of success, but they are some of the most important. Think about your own experience. What laws have you discovered that apply across circumstance and situations? To put it differently, what laws of success have you discovered inadvertently by breaking them?

Being an outlaw of success is a metaphor about breaking through the mediocrity that surrounds us and pushing the limits of achievement. Being an outlaw of success is about bending or breaking the rules, for sure. But it is also about keeping the laws of success as a means of living life fully.

Abraham Maslow said, "The unhappiness, unease and unrest in the world today are caused by people living far below their capacity."

To live below your capacity is the greatest crime of all. Racking up an impressive list of accomplishments that don't bring you fulfillment or keep your juices flowing makes for a long and uncomfortable life—it's probably the second greatest crime. Instead, go thundering across the ridge line and choose your trail with the wind in your hair and your hands on the reins. The outlaw goes where few have dared to try. You will know when you've joined the company of outlaws when you're achieving exceptional success and you're having fun doing it. You will also discover that there is honor among outlaws—they know more than anyone does what it takes to achieve greatness and they appreciate the effort it takes to implement the laws of success.

It's time to hit the trail of success. Ride hard and live free.

MARK SANBORN, CSP, CPAE

Because of his ability to educate and entertain simultaneously, Mark Sanborn is known internationally as *the high content speaker who motivates*. Mark presents 90-100 programs annually on leadership, teambuilding, customer service and mastering change.

His clients include Airtouch Cellular, BMW Financial, Exxon, Hewlett Packard, Mortons of Chicago, New York Life, Price Costco, and ServiceMaster. Mark is the author or coauthor of seven books, including *Teambuilt: Making Teamwork Work, Sanborn On Success*, and *Meditations for the Road Warrior*. He has also authored 20 videos and numerous audio training programs.

Clients appreciate that Mark does the research necessary to understand their needs and tailors his presentation to meet their objectives. Leslie Kvasnicka of the Society of Quality Assurance wrote, "You took time to understand our organization and its members. You made your presentation seem to be designed specifically for us and we loved it!"

In 1995 *Presentations* magazine featured Mark as one of five "Masters of the Microphone." Mark has earned the Certified Speaking Professional designation and is a member of the exclusive Speaker Hall of Fame.

His program titles include:

- **The Fred Factor:** *Reinventing Your Business & Life Through Personal Leadership.*

- **High Impact Leadership**

- **The 10 Commandments of Customer Service**

- **Making Teamwork Work**

- **Mastering Change**

Mark Sanborn Order Form

How To Live The American Dream
  (one hour motivational video) $99
How To Manage Your Time, Energy & Relationships
  (2 audios) $20
The Fred Factor: Reinventing Your Business & Your
  Life Through Personal Leadership *(audio)* $10
Mastering Change *(2 one hour videos)* $199
Speak Like a Pro *(4 audio cassettes)* $49
The 10 Commandments of Customer Service
  (audio cassette) $10
Teambuilding: How To Manage & Motivate People
  (4 audios) $49
Teambuilding: How To Manage & Motivate People
  (2 videos) $249
High Impact Leadership *(4 audios)* $49
High Impact Leadership *(3 videos)* $249
Teambuilding workbooks .... $5 ea.
High Impact Leadership workbooks .... $5 ea.
Empowerment: Unleashing the Potential of
  Performance *(video)* $159
Teambuilt: Making Teamwork Work *(book)* $12.95
Sanborn On Success *(book)* $8.95
Meditations for the Road Warrior *(book)* $14.95
Outlaw Wisdom *(book)* $9.95
The Outlaws Of Success *(book)* $12.95

Please add $5.00 Shipping & Handling

To order or for more information about Mark's books, tapes,
speeches and training sessions contact:

Sanborn & Associates, Inc.
818 E. Summer Drive
Highlands Ranch, CO 80126
(800) 650-3343 • Fax (303) 683-0825
email: MarkSpeaks@aol.com
http://www.marksanborn.com

CHAPTER 5

NEGOTIATION...
OUTLAW STYLE

■ ■

by John Patrick Dolan, CSP, CPAE

Negotiation...
Outlaw Style

by John Patrick Dolan, CSP, CPAE

■■■■■■■■■■■■■■■■■■■■■■■■■■

Six Steps For Negotiation Preparation

The most commonly overlooked aspect of negotiation is preparation. We say things like, "We're just in the negotiation stage of the deal..."

There is no more profitable expenditure of time than the time spent preparing to negotiate. Here's your checklist:

1. Know what you want and don't want...

Most of us have a general idea of what we want or want to avoid in a deal. Unfortunately, general objectives tend to render general results...leading to second guessing and dissatisfaction.

Instead, write a paragraph describing in detail what you want and don't want from the transaction, then, edit this description furiously until it is laser focused and precise.

When we are crystal clear on our objective(s) and rationale(s) for their acquisition, we are most likely to achieve desired results.

2. Know what your counterpart wants and doesn't want...

Now do the same for your counterpart. Write the description of what your opposite is looking for and seeking to avoid.

This exercise tends to be a real stumper...and eventually a real eye-opener. Knowing our counterpart's goals, objectives, and sought after results helps us see commonalities that lead to creative solutions.

3. Know what concessions you are willing to give...

What must you absolutely achieve to consummate a successful bargain? What terms, conditions, extras could you live without? Every great negotiator knows there must be give and take on both sides for agreements that make sense.

4. Know your alternatives...

Remember when you bought your first car? Mine was a 1956 T-Bird. The guy I bought mine from told me, "I like you and want to sell you the car...but there's another person coming over in 30 minutes who also wants the car." Wow, did the dynamics of the negotiation shift on the spot. Having an alternative vendor or supplier really helps your level of confidence.

5. Know your counterpart and your subject matter...

A lot of information is available to us on personality styles, body language, and neuro-linguistic programming. Remember transactions take place between people...and people view the same facts and appeals differently. Subject matter is simple...Know it cold—there is no excuse for being ill informed...and lost credibility is rarely recovered.

6. Rehearse

You know how to get to Carnegie Hall! It's the same road to negotiation success—Practice—Practice—Practice! Attend swap meets and flea markets...They are wonderful opportunities to sharpen you skills. Remember use it or lose it!

Most negotiators rarely, if ever, thoroughly prepare to negotiate. But this is the magic! Try this checklist before you negotiate...Your returns will improve dramatically.

Negotiating With Style

"The Platinum Rule"

We all know the golden rule...*Do unto others as you would have them do unto you.* Dr. Tony Alessandra in his book, *The Platinum Rule* (1996 Warner Books) says there is a better way...*Do unto others as they want to be done unto.*

How does this relate to negotiation? Quite simply we negotiate with **people** or groups of people. As the personality styles of our counterparts vary, so must we vary our approaches to different people. We can review the wonderful information in Dr. Alessandra's book and then make some decisions as to our particular approach with particular personalities.

Different people observe, interpret, and act on information differently.

Here is a short summary of the four styles that Dr. Alessandra discusses in his book:

- **Directors**—Football coaches, drill sergeants, dictators. Directors are challenge oriented take-charge decision makers. Achievement and success are defined by overcoming obstacles and realizing accomplishments.

- **Socializer**—Are "people" people. PR directors, sales people, actors, and speakers. Appreciation and recognition are what the socializer seeks. Time spent *schmoozing* is time well spent.
- **Relaters**—Friendly and reliable. Relaters are team players who exercise extreme patience in difficult times and work for the long term gain.
- **Thinkers**—Serious, analytical people with long term goals. They ponder choices until they have all the information and analysis to make a proper, well thought out decision.

How each style tends to operate and how to negotiate with each is critical to the overall success in our negotiations.

Directors like to take action...to accept challenges...to achieve and accomplish...fear being "soft." The best way to negotiate with a director is to offer him or her a selection of several potential alternatives and a deadline. Let them choose. They will feel "in charge" and if you're careful in designing the potential alternatives you will get what you want.

The **Socializer** wants to "shoot the breeze"...have fun...make a favorable impression...speak with an articulate style. They fear being disliked. They want you to be their friend...ask them about themselves...appreciate their wit. If they like you and believe you like them they will do business with you and make you a great deal.

Relaters want tranquility and stability...They desire a stable work environment...They like to sit or stay in one place. They want predictability and reliability in any important transaction. They do not like surprises, changes, or modifications without advance notice. To successfully negotiate with the relater we need to emphasize our trustworthiness and the predictable, reliable nature of the transaction. Following the step-by-step process to predictable reliable results works the best here.

Thinkers are fact-oriented and take pride on being meticulous. They want to know how things work and want time to analyze and organize tasks. Their work is high quality, although sometimes they take longer than we would like for them to take. They can be perceived as over critical and sometimes insensitive. Their biggest fear is being wrong. They would rather not make a decision than to make a poor or incorrect (irrational) decision.

Negotiating is a person to person process.

Have fun the next time you negotiate by observing carefully the personality style cues exhibited by your counterpart(s).

Being sensitive to personality orientation can really increase our successes, reduce friction, and lead us to better agreements.

Try it...You'll be negotiating with style!

Dealing with Difficult Negotiators

Outrageous Behavior

Screaming, yelling, ranting, raving, cursing, throwing items across the table, hanging up the phone in your ear...Many of us have difficulty with negotiators who do these things.

These outrageous behaviors can shake us up, intimidate, scare, or upset us.

Why? The most common explanation is that our *fight-flight* response is evoked. *Fighting* rarely gets us moving toward a meaningful agreement. *Fright* can cause us to make compromises or give concessions we would otherwise never entertain.

Why Do They Do It?

Why do some negotiators rely on outrageous behavior to get their way? Because they *can*...or because they *have* in the past.

But, we don't have to allow this behavior to cause us to give in.

Feigned Emotion

Some negotiators act as if they are emotionally upset when they really are not.

Usually, this negotiator is the sophisticated, high level, *manipulator* who is looking for an advantage. His intention is calculated. The results sought are pre-planned.

Tantrum Behavior

The overwhelming majority of *screamers* are just stuck in a *tantrum behavior pattern*. As a child they threw tantrums and got what they wanted. As an adolescent they pressed the bounds of behavior. As an adult, they just act like big babies who *must have what they want*!

What Can We Do?

Whether the outrageous behavior is fake or real, we can deal with it without making serious compromises.

Silence is first. Not engaging a *screamer*…letting the screamer go uninterrupted works many times. Some negotiators simply want to be heard. Genuinely upset, some negotiators become quiet compliant *after* they have vented. In fact, sometimes the *boomerang* affect can set in…that is, a screamer after venting, will accept whatever is offered, and may even give more than expected.

Avoid Taunts. Many times we fall into taunting behavior as a defense. "Are you finished?"…"Yell a little louder!"…"Who do you think you are talking to?" These responses do not help. We must avoid these taunts, secure in the knowledge that our objective of a negotiated agreement is primary.

Mirror Behavior. This probably sounds contradictory (and probably is) but sometimes *shouting back* can be the answer. This technique has limited utility but when effective is best used as an *out of character* response. People who almost never yell can use mirroring effectively on really important issues.

Feel, Felt, Found. The feel, felt, found technique works well with outrageous behavior because at its core this techinique seems to validate the unaccepted behavior...and then provides enlightenment. **Feel**..."I understand how you feel." This is the validation or commiseration phase. **Felt**..."Many people in your position would have felt the same way." This is the generalization phase. Your irate counterpart is in league with many other (ill-informed) people. **Found**..."But understanding...(Point A, B, C)...most people have found our position is quite reasonable." The A and B, and C are the features, benefits, and additional appeals that support our position.

Positive Outrageous Behavior. Give them a reason to laugh. Goofy behavior, funny statements and strange responses that cause laughter can many times disarm the worst *tantrum behavior pattern.*

Good luck dealing with difficult negotiators...we all need it!

Spitting in Your Soup

During the 1950's Korean Conflict, six American GI's were assigned to a housing unit. Fighting had calmed down, so they found themselves living in close quarters with extra time on their hands.

Predictably, they soon started playing practical jokes on each other...sneaking up on each other, rubber snake tricks, etc.

Quickly tiring of these games, they started pulling these little pranks on their houseboy Wan. They liked this good natured Korean boy—happy to have the job—and figured they'd include him in their practical jokes.

They would tie his boots together while he was sleeping and make loud clanging noises with their mess kits. Wan would jump up, thinking the enemy was attacking, and fall right on his face. Ha Ha!

They'd hang a bucket of water above his door and place a tripcord in the threshold. Then, they would call Wan into the room, and watch him get drenched.

One day the soldiers were sitting around drinking, and someone commented that Wan seemed a little down. They quickly realized that the cause of Wan's depression was the practical jokes they had been playing. They had only meant to make him feel included, but obviously he only felt humiliated. The soldiers apologized and promised never to do it again.

Wan's quick reply was "OK, GI...then I'll stop spitting in your soup." Gross but poignant.

Anytime we deal with others in an unethical, or manipulative manner, we risk the same fate as our GI friends.

Maintaining an attitude of integrity, ethics, and fair dealing in any negotiation is not only the right thing to do...it's the least costly in the long run.

Remember what mom said..."Be nice..." Not only is mature adult conduct in negotiations its own reward...You'll avoid people *spitting in your soup*.

"Let's Just Split It Down The Middle"

Everybody's Heard of It

If there's one thing we all know about negotiation it's the "Split it down the middle" (SIDTM) technique. You're very close on the purchase of your first car (in my case a 1956 Thunderbird in 1966), the difference between what the seller is asking [$850 for the T-bird] and what the buyer is offering [$750 is what I'd offered], and so one party offers and the other party accepts an inducement to "split it down the middle."

Everybody's Used It

In the realm of give and take it's almost genetic. On every continent, in every culture, in every kind of transaction the SIDTM technique is known and practiced.

What Makes it Attractive?

Why does SIDTM work? What dimensions of this technique cause it to be so universally embraced?

Fairness is first. The element of fairness in SIDTM is extant in the fact that both parties give and both parties get something. The SIDTM compromise works for both parties. We obtain a concession...we grant a concession. What could be more fair?

Time savings is also an important and valuable consideration in SIDTM. We all have an internal time clock running within our gut. There comes a juncture in many negotiations when we conclude the expenditure of additional time on a particular transaction becomes counterproductive...Let's just "split it down the middle and get this thing over with!"

Finally, SIDTM is the transition from negotiation to performance. The closure provided allows us to begin to receive the benefit of our bargains.

It's a Great Tactic, an Awful Strategy

This wonderful tactic, however, can lead us into an awful strategy. Why? It seems as though the combination of an almost universal death of negotiation training and the almost universal knowledge of SIDTM have resulted in a default strategy...

When our strategy is to "split the difference" between our offer and our counterpart's offer it naturally follows that we would establish a relatively extreme position. Since we know we will not get what we ask for...we ask for a lot more than we really think is reasonable.

Unless our counterpart is ignorant, the natural response to our extreme position is to state an equally extreme position in the opposite direction.

Now what? We expend tremendous amounts of energy defending our clearly extreme position. Until when? Until a mutually perceived deadline. Then what? Some form of SIDTM behavior with predictable distasteful results.

The buyer returns to his or her office and grouses "I could have bought for less if I'd held out a little longer." The seller returns to his or her office and complains "I could have sold for more if I'd held out a little longer."

What an awful strategy! We establish extreme positions, we defend these silly positions until some perceived deadline. Then we split the difference in some fashion with predictable dissatisfaction. There must be a better way!

Reject the Strategy...Retain the Tactic

The source of our solution is to understand the difference between the kinds of issues presented in any particular negotiation scenario. Principle issues and positional issues.

SIDTM is most useful in positional negotiation. However, principle negotiation should logically come first.

Fisher and Ury in their wonderful book *Getting to Yes* provide a concise explanation of the difference between **principle** and **positional** issues. The book is a tremendous addition to your negotiation library.

In short, principle issues reflect the values, objections, decisions, and interests we feel support our contemplated transactions. Positional issues represent the actual amount, place, time, or concessionary equilibrium we finally reach.

Sister is at home doing her homework at the kitchen table. Brother comes home and turns on his "Offspring" CD at the 150 decibel level.

Her position..."Turn that off! I can't do my homework with all that noise."

His position..."I live here too and I want to listen to my music!"

This is a common set of stand-off positions with no real apparent compromise.

Brother and sister could agree to specific times for homework and music listening. Mom and dad could eject one or both of them from the house. However, neither of these solutions offers long term satisfaction.

They could split it down the middle ... turn the music down half-way. However, this situation is only a partial resolution of their differences. The SIDTM solution builds in the seeds of mistrust.

If he leaves the living room she goes in and turns the music down. When he comes back he notices the reduced volume level and turns the music back up... not to the previous level but to an even higher level.

She wants silence. He wants to listen to real loud music. How can they both get what they want?

Headphones! Headphones allow both parties to have all of what they are looking for in this everyday example of give and take.

If we can become clear as to what we really want in a transaction and why we want it, and if we can become clear as to what our counterpart wants, and why; then, a "headphones" type solution is highly probable.

Application of the New Strategy

In sales and marketing this new principle driven strategy is seen in the consultative selling approach. We learn what our customers want rather than simply selling them what we have.

When our customers complain we make an in-depth inquiry into the sources of dissatisfaction rather than simply waving a policy manual at them.

When we seek to negotiate behavior in the workplace we honestly attempt to understand the reasons behind our employees conduct rather than making threats about their continued employment.

A "headphones" type solution is potentially possible in almost every negotiation scenario. But, we need to spend time and effort working toward that solution. If not, we fall back into the old patterns.

SIDTM is a great tactic...but it's a lousy strategy.

By the way, I bought the T-Bird for $800 and sold it two years later for $1,200...thought I was a genius! I wish I still owned that car today.

Thrift Stores, Movies, And Mom

We Negotiate Every Day

Give and take techniques abound all around us. Thrift stores, movies, and mom give us several opportunities to see everyday negotiation action.

Wincing, Limited Authority, False Deadlines

Go to your local thrift store, flea market, or swap meet. Practice your negotiation techniques while buying a cheesy Hawaiian shirt. Here's how it goes…

Merchant: "May I help you sir or madam?"

You: "Why yes, how much is this cheesy Hawaiian shirt?"

Merchant; "Ten dollars."

You: "Ten dollars!" (A wince, followed by silence)

Merchant: "How about eight dollars?"

You: "Eight dollars!" (Another wince) "My mom said I could only spend $5.00 on any cheesy Hawaiian shirt I wanted." (Limited authority)

Merchant: "Five dollars!" (Another wince)

You: "Yes, and we have to leave for home in five minutes." (False deadline)

Merchant: "Well, okay kid, I'll let you have it for five dollars."

You: "Ah, great," you say to yourself, "I really got him."

Merchant: (To himself) "That's the most I've gotten for one of these dogs in months!"

Silence In The Movies

Weekend at Bernie's is a great example of silence in negotiation. Although Bernie is dead, nobody seems to notice. While propped up on a sofa at a party, dead Bernie receives an offer to buy his Porsche for $35,000.

Bernie is silent. Minutes later he is offered $40,000. Bernie still says nothing. Then he is offered $45,000. More silence. Even when the offer tops $55,000, Bernie still says nothing. If we acted more like Bernie, we'd put a lot more life in our negotiations.

In *Glengarry Glen Ross*, there is a scene where Al Pacino loses a sale because Kevin Spacey volunteers information in front of Pacino's client without knowing the details of the negotiations. Pacino later tells Spacey, *"You never open your mouth until you know what the shot is."* Larry Winget, a Tulsa, Oklahoma based motivational speaker, says that you never volunteer unsolicited information because it's often used in objections later on.

Mom Knows Best (Pressure Technique)

Have you ever had a pushy person try to pressure you into a quick decision on an important matter? Yielding to this kind of pressure (which is really just another false deadline) can be disastrous.

Our moms knew this when we were kids. Remember when we would relentlessly badger our moms for a quick answer to a seemingly monumental problem? Mom would say, "If I have to answer you now the answer has to be **no.** But, if you give me some time to think about it, the answer might be **yes.**"

Smart kids are usually willing to let up a little bit in return for the potential of a positive outcome.

This technique works great with pushy adults…bosses, employees, spouses, etc. Try it. Mom knows best.

Keep your eyes open…every day we are exposed to and impacted by negotiation techniques all around us.

The wise negotiator is a keen observer and an aggressive adapter of effective techniques occurring in his or her presence.

The Gender Blenders—How Successful Men And Women Mix-It-Up In Negotiation

Men and women have been talking to each other, past each other and at each other ever since Adam became separated from his rib and the first gender gap was opened.

Our early ancestors settled on a division of labor, dictated largely by biological necessity: The women bore the children and carried within their bosoms their infants' first food supply. Hence, Mama stayed home with the kids while Papa went hunting Mastodons and fighting bad guys from other tribes.

Mama dug up roots and picked berries to go with the meaty victuals Papa brought home, but outside the Clan of the Cave Bear, she was an observer, not a participant in the hunt.

From early history, boys and girls grew up in separate cultures, schooled in separate roles. Not surprisingly, then, men and women developed identifiable styles of communication. Papa's language was the language of the hunt and the fight; the language of competition. Mama's language was the language of hearth and home; of nurturing and cooperation. It should not surprise us that men and women frequently misunderstand one another, even in everyday communications.

Even into modern times, girls were expected to learn the arts of housekeeping— cooking, sewing, child-rearing—while boys were expected to learn trades or enter the professions. Men were strong and assertive while women were beautiful and submissive.

Some women did embark on careers, but only those reserved for the "fairer sex": teaching, nursing, and occasionally writing.

But whatever role they chose, they were expected to be women first—virtuous, yielding, dainty and pretty.

Throughout history, the strongest have made the rules, and until modern times the strong were the people with the muscles and agility—which meant the men.

Women could negotiate, but only from positions of weakness, since men made the laws and had the brawn to enforce them.

Today strength still prevails, but power is no longer measured by the size of your biceps. Technology has leveled the playing field so that women can fly airplanes, drive 18-wheelers, and operate construction cranes as skillfully as men.

They can also program computers, chart market trends and plot corporate strategies with all the finesse that men can muster. They are joining the men in the hunt, and when the men try to force them away, they don't have to defend their status with a club; they can wield the law instead.

Increasingly, women are taking their places at corporate tables as fully participating executives. They are interacting with men as equals, not as subordinates.

The "man's world" that used to exist has been evaporating—sometimes slowly, to be sure—ever since women won the right to vote.

Women have more than doubled their representation in non-clerical white-collar jobs in American companies since the 1960's, and now occupy almost half these positions. But a 1994 survey by the Wall Street Journal showed that women still held less than a third of the managerial jobs in the 38,059 companies that reported to the U.S. Equal Employment Opportunity Commission in 1992, the latest year for which data were available. And among 200 of the nation's biggest companies analyzed by the Journal, women held just one-fourth of the jobs classified by the EEOC as "officials and managers"—a broad category that includes a wide variety of supervisory posts, from the manager of the janitorial service to the CEO of the company.

At the vice presidential level, women made up an even smaller percentage—less than 5% in 1990, according to Catalyst, a nonprofit research group in New York that studies women in business.

Many women get the feeling that this preponderance of males in top positions creates a management culture that is hostile to females.

Companies that do succeed in populating their executive suites with a sizable female contingent find that it becomes easier to attract able women.

The Sara Lee Corp. began hiring women into high-level jobs during the 1980's and, as The Journal put it, "watched the cultural changes trickle down." The newspaper quoted Gary Grom, senior vice president of human resources: "The more women in top management jobs, the more women are attracted to them." The reason this is true is that women find it easier to relate to other women and men find it easier to relate to other men.

Women often don't fit into the corporate culture—which was developed by and for men.

Wells Fargo is a company that has succeeded in changing their corporate cultures into a blend of genders. By the early '90's, about two-thirds of its management people were women. By 1992, seven of the 38 executive vice presidents and 19 of the 108 senior vice presidents were women.

Companies such as Sara Lee and Wells Fargo demonstrate that when a certain critical mass is achieved, the genders can form a successful blend.

The ideal situation—the one toward which we hope we are moving—would be a work force populated equally by men and women at all levels, with equal opportunity for all.

In such an environment, men and women would develop a common language based upon common activities. A language in which the best features of both are blended.

This gender-blended language will enable men and women to communicate precisely and comfortably with one another—across the conference table, and across the dinner table...and gender-blending is already a work in progress.

World Class Negotiation...Working Door To Door In The Global Village

Sydney, Australia was the destination. Quantas Flight AF008 (LAX to Sydney nonstop) was the particular flight. 58H was my seat assignment...in Economy? Yes, Economy happens.

I'd tried all my best techniques with the counter attendant but to no avail. Wearing a suit to appear the perfect upgrade candidate, smiling, commiserating with her obviously heavy workload, volunteering to move up to business or first class to help better distribute weight throughout the aircraft. Nothing worked.

No one gets what they want every time...Even Mr. Negotiator. However, the real lesson here is never give up.

While the obvious objective of an upgrade was not obtained, the seat between myself and the fellow next to me was however, blocked (unoccupied) by the counter attendant. And it was a full flight.

Every adversity offers an equal or greater opportunity! The reputation of this mantra helped me to accept my fate...Seat H, Row 58 in Economy.

Polite introductions were exchanged between myself and my fellow occupant (Bob) of Row 58 (Right side Economy on a 747-400 aircraft).

Through three meal services, two bar services, and four feature films, we became better acquainted.

It turns out Bob was a writer from The New York Times traveling through Sydney to Papua, New Guinea. His assignment was to write an article on travel and leisure.

By exchanging information and references, Bob and I made a great deal on our (LawTalk™ is our company) new legal lifestyle magazine. In return, I provided him with suggestions on how to navigate through Customs and Immigration in Sydney, and what sights to see before he traveled north to the jungle.

We negotiate everyday. And, we never know when the use of our give-and-take talents will result in an unforeseen long term benefit.

The Southern Cross Hotel in Sydney is a great place. The staff at the Southern Cross is so congenial that I choose to stay there each time I travel to Sydney.

"This is a suite, isn't it?"

I received a suite for the same price as a regular room.

Always ask for an upgrade when you book your hotel reservation and again when you check in.

After a week of heavy negotiation on several business deals, it was time to go home. Seat 58H was bad enough. On my return flight, I convinced the counter attendant to allocate me seat 48H (Bulkhead exit row). More leg room! (I thought.) Unfortunately, 48H is also the area where people congregate waiting for an opportunity to use the bathroom. "Be careful what you ask for because you just might get it!" was my new mantra.

Remember, world class negotiation techniques are powerful tools but we should always keep in mind that we use these techniques door-to-door...one person at a time.

An Oral Contract Isn't Worth The Paper It's Written On

Friends and colleagues ask me all the time, "John what kinds of things should I include in my written contract...for a car? ...for a new home purchase? ...in a business transaction?"

I have always found it helpful to use a checklist as a reminder of potential issues that should be considered.

Here are some of the things on my checklist that may be useful to you. The entire checklist can be found in the book, *How to Build a More Lucrative Law Practice* by Noel Stevenson.

Definitions: Define any terms used in the contract which are open to interpretation, but remember that definitions are dangerous.

Parties: Names and addresses of parties. Avoid using "party of the first part," "party of the second part." Instead, identify parties by "Smith" and Jones," "buyer" and "seller" or "Lessor" and "Lessee," "Exclusive Agent."

Legal Status: Ascertain the marital or legal status of the parties.

Date of Execution: The date of the contract. It is advisable to avoid the use of an "as of" date, as it indicates that the contract was not signed on that date.

Effective Date: The effective date of the contract.

Arbitration: Provision for arbitration disputes.

Age and Competence: Are the parties competent to contract? It isn't advisable to rely on appearances, sometimes an eighteen year old looks and acts over twenty-one. As for mental competency, usually all one can do is observe and hope for the best.

Jurisdiction: Consider including a recital of the law of what jurisdiction should apply to the contract.

Time is of the Essence: Is it advisable to provide that time is of the essence of the contract?

Performance Duties: Include in specific terms what performance each of the parties is liable for and the time when each obligation is to be performed.

Future Changes to the Law: Make provisions for any future change of the law or administrative regulations which would affect the parties.

Performance—Reason for Delays in: Make provisions for strikes, acts of war, acts of God, or any other catastrophes which prevent or delay performances of one of the parties.

Consideration: What is the consideration of the contract?

Modification: Provide that any modification of the contract must be in writing.

Payment of Money: State the time and place of payment of any money.

Damages—Default: Provide for damages, if any should be paid, in case of the default of a party.

Cancellation—Provision for: If any party to the contract has a right to cancel the contract, include provision for such cancellation.

Paragraph Headings: Consider including paragraph headings such as "Insurance," "Notices," "Covenant Not to Complete." If these paragraph headings are included, provide in the contract that these subject headings are for the sake of convenience and are not a part of the contract.

Conclusion

Good luck with your agreements. Remember the most important thing in writing an agreement is that it should be designed to provide for real or potential ambiguities and difficulties...not for litigation. Unless your contract concerns high six-figure agreements, you should stay away from lawyers and litigation...it's too expensive...*trust me!* Remember, *every one of these issues is negotiable.* Use this checklist and you will be able to *Negotiate like the Pros*™.

WANTED

JOHN PATRICK DOLAN

JOHN PATRICK DOLAN
CSP, CPAE

John Patrick Dolan, one of the world's leading authorities on negotiation, speaks from experience. Not only has he been a trial attorney for nearly 20 years, he's an accredited legal education provider for critical negotiating skills to the United States legal community. While attending law school he worked as a licensed stock broker for Merrill Lynch. During this time he also received and insurance brokers license. John Patrick Dolan is currently CEO of *LawTalk*™, a consulting firm that provides keynote speeches and training programs for business and legal professionals. John obtained his Bachelor of Arts degrees in Speech Communication and Political Science from California State University, Fullerton as well as a Doctor of Law degree from WSU College of Law.

The National Speakers Association recently presented John Patrick Dolan with the coveted Council of Peers Award for Excellence based on his uniqueness of style, delivery, reputation, professionalism and ability to relate to all audiences. This, combined with his book *Negotiate Like The Pros*, and his audio and video programs make him one of the most sought after

speakers on the topic of negotiation throughout the
United States and the English speaking world.

John Patrick Dolan has presented custom in-house
programs, seminars and keynote speeches to organizations
as diverse as the Texas Rangers, the National Association
of Music Merchants, and Apple Computer. Clients say
this about John: the American Bar Association — "I have
had virtually everyone go out of their way to call and tell
me how much they enjoyed and profited from your
negotiation training"; Meeting Planners International —
"Most of the comments were from meeting planners
telling me that this was the best meeting we've had in a
long time," National Society for Healthcare Foodservice
Management — "Thank you for contributing to the
success of our conference. When I think of negotiating, I
will think of John Patrick Dolan!"

For a press kit or booking information contact:

LawTalk™
714-257-3414 or 800-859-0888
Fax: 714-257-3424
E-mail: Lawtalkcle@aol.com

John Patrick Dolan Order Form

Product	Description	Qty	Price	S/H	Total
Books					
The Outlaws Of Success	Book (156 pages)		$12.95	$2.00	
Outlaw Wisdom	Book (112 pages)		$ 9.95	$2.00	
Negotiate like the Pros™	Autographed Book		$11.00	$2.00	
Negotiate like the Pros™	Autographed Book Single Tape		$20.00	$2.00	
Leadership Strategies	Book (228 pages)		$32.95	$3.00	
Movers & Shakers	Book (336 pages)		$32.95	$3.00	
Audio/Video					
Negotiate like the Pros™ The Original	6 Audio Tapes Autographed Book		$79.95	$4.00	
Negotiate like the Pros™ Live Audio Workshop	6 Audio Tapes Autographed Book Workbook		$79.95	$4.00	
Negotiate like the Pros™ Live Video Workshop	4 Video Tapes Workbook		$249.95	$7.50	
Negotiate like the Pros™ Live Workshop Package	6 Audio Tapes 4 Volume Video Workbook Autographed Book		$399.95	$10.00	
T-Shirts	Negotiate like the Pros™ T-shirt		$20.00	$4.00	
				TOTAL ORDER	

Name _____ Date _____

Company _____

STREET Address _____

City/Province _____

Zip/Postal Code _____ Country _____ Day Phone _____

Method of Payment: ☐ AMEX ☐ VISA ☐ Mastercard ☐ Check/Money Order Enclosed

Card No. | | | | | | | | | | | | | | | | |

Exp. date _____ Signature _____

or mail to:
LawTalk™

Fax to: 714 257-3424   555 Pointe Drive, Building 3, Ste 302
Brea, CA 92821-3651